More praise for *The Music Room*

"A haunting lament for a life that could have been and the love that remained for a broken mind. I read it and hugged my children afterwards." —Amanda Foreman, author of *Georgiana, Duchess of Devonshire*

"Masterful—this is a book of such quivering tenderness and beauty that it's as if the author played it on the strings of his family's generous heart. In its execution, one thinks of Evelyn Waugh. In its great warmth and generosity, I am reminded of the films of Julian Schnabel. In its psychological depth and restraint, it recalls Kazuo Ishiguro."

—Alexandra Fuller, author of *The Legend of Colton H. Bryant* and *Don't Let's Go to the Dogs Tonight*

"This book is a marvel. Like the best poetry, its lucid, simple narrative is able to achieve myriad things at once, and Fiennes enables his readers to enlarge their own sympathies. He not only teaches us to understand a much-misunderstood disease but fills us with gratitude for the intricate workings of the human mind, in which the physical and spiritual, past and present inform, pervade, and enrich each other."

—Karen Armstrong, author of *The Spiral Staircase* and *A History of God*

"Searing melancholy and quiet exuberance are twined with scholarship in this elegant book, written with an infinite restraint that makes the emotionally charged contents almost unbearably poignant."

—Andrew Solomon, author of *The Noonday Demon*

"Astute and tender . . . a thoughtful and lyrical account of an extraordinary childhood. . . . Fiennes is an unusually skilled writer."

—*The Guardian*

"*The Music Room* is exemplary."

—*The Telegraph*

"In his gentle, poetic voice Mr. Fiennes intersperses childhood scenes with sections about the history of the study of the brain and of epilepsy."

—Sarah Lyall, *New York Times*

"*The Music Room* is humane rather than melodramatic, a lovely memoir rich with poignancy of family and place."

—*Wall Street Journal*

"An artful memory piece about a unique home life."

—*Kirkus Reviews*

THE MUSIC ROOM

Also by William Fiennes

THE SNOW GEESE

WILLIAM FIENNES

o

THE MUSIC ROOM

W. W. NORTON & COMPANY
New York • London

Copyright © 2009 by William Fiennes
First American Edition 2009

For information about permission to reproduce selections from this book,
write to Permissions, W. W. Norton & Company, Inc.,
500 Fifth Avenue, New York, NY 10110

For information about special discounts for bulk purchases, please contact
W. W. Norton Special Sales at specialsales@wwnorton.com or 800-233-4830

Manufacturing by Courier Westford
Production manager: Julia Druskin

Library of Congress Cataloging-in-Publication Data

Fiennes, William.
The music room / William Fiennes.—1st American ed.
p. cm.
Also published: London : Picador, 2009.
ISBN 978-0-393-07258-7 (hardcover)
1. Fiennes, William—Childhood and youth. 2. Fiennes, William—Family. 3. Fiennes, William—
Homes and haunts—England—Banbury Region (Oxfordshire) 4. Broughton Castle (England)
5. Brothers—England—Biography. 6. Epileptics—England—Biography.
7. Banbury Region (Oxfordshire, England)—Biography. I. Title.
CT788.F436A3 2009
942.5'7086092—dc22
[B]
2009018457

ISBN 978-0-393-33878-2 pbk.

W. W. Norton & Company, Inc.
500 Fifth Avenue, New York, N.Y. 10110
www.wwnorton.com

W. W. Norton & Company Ltd.
Castle House, 75/76 Wells Street, London W1T 3QT

1 2 3 4 5 6 7 8 9 0

THE MUSIC ROOM

ONE

THE SCHOOL ASSEMBLY HALL was closed for renovations and on Sundays we walked to a church for our weekly service. We spread rumours along pews and daydreamed through sermons until one visiting preacher secured our attention by hoisting a bag onto the pulpit rim – a scuffed black leather bag with accordion pleats at each end, a bag a doctor might take on night visits – and unpacking metal stands and clamps we recognized from science labs, and various jars and packages he ranged along the shelf in front of him. He was in his fifties, dressed in a grey suit and a black shirt with a white dog collar, and he didn't say anything while preparing his equipment, tightening a clamp on a retort stand, fixing a cardboard tube between the jaws. He struck a match; a fuse caught and sizzled; he shook the match out and stepped back to watch the flame. Then we understood that what he'd clamped to the stand was a firework. The tube flared with a soft, liquid rush, sparks and white embers falling to the stone floor, the preacher's spectacles glinting in the brightness. The fountain died with a last sputter like someone clearing their throat, the after-image burning in our eyes.

'Light,' the preacher said.

o

Our house was almost seven hundred years old, a medieval beginning transformed in the sixteenth century into a Tudor stately home, a castle surrounded by a broad moat, with woods, farmland and a landscaped park on the far side, and a gatehouse tower guarding the two-arched stone bridge, the island's only point of access and departure.

The gatehouse doors hung on rusty iron hinges, grids of sun-bleached vertical and cross beams like the gates of an ancient city, a Troy or Jericho, creaking like ships as you manoeuvred them. I pushed my hand deep into the keyhole to feel the lock tumblers, and climbed the waffle pattern of oak beams until my strength gave out; I imagined cauldrons of boiling oil tipped through the trapdoor on intruders; I gazed up at the flagpole turret, a canvas flag of blue and white quadrants, gold lions and black moles and chevrons rippling overhead, jackdaws clacking like snooker balls.

When the gates were closed it was as if the house had picked up a shield, but they were almost always open. My father worried for the strength of the hinges and didn't want to stress them. The gatehouse was a rugged keep with arrow-slit windows and a spiral staircase of cold stone that turned through zones of light and shadow to a leaded roof, the moat far below, a heron stooped like an Anglepoise on the near bank, moorhens legging it across the grass. My mother painted Turtle and Pearce flag bunting on the parquet floor by the upright piano; my father carried the new flag up the gatehouse stairs; I followed him onto the roof, watching as he propped the ladder against turret battlements and began to climb. He attached the flag by duffel-coat toggles and when he raised it the canvas unfurled with flame-like rip and putter, blue and white quarters flush to the wind.

o

Richard was the eldest, eleven years older than me, eighteen months older than Martin and Susannah, the twins. My father's parents had died within ten days of each other not long before I was born, and my family had moved from their village house to the estate passed down through my father's ancestors since the fourteenth century.

Beyond the churchyard a path of irregular flagstones joined by seams of moss and grass led past the orchard to the road, a wrought-iron gate hanging off-kilter on the far side. Sometimes I opened the gate and took the gravel path uphill through a scrubby wasteland district of nettles and elder bushes. The country flattened off and you came to a stockade of iron railings tipped with spear-points, a kissing-gate that groaned when you disturbed it. The graveyard backed into farmland, a sea of wheat pressing against the railings, trees busy with wrens and chaffinches on the other three sides, floral tributes slumped against the headstones. My grandparents and great-uncles and aunts were buried here; a newer stone beside them marked the grave of my brother Thomas, too soon for lichens or mosses to have got started.

My father kept a black-and-white photograph of him in a leather frame by his bed, and another next to the lamp on his desk; my mother had the same photograph under the glass top of her dressing-table: a boy standing on a hillside, not quite three years old, hair teased by wind, hands clasped in front of his chest, looking away into unrevealed distances. He looked like both of my brothers and me, all at once. Sometimes I stood close to the photograph – I was always careful not to touch it – and concentrated on Thomas, looking for small changes in his expression, trying to imagine him in three dimensions, walking into the kitchen or across the lawn. I wanted to hear his voice.

I knew what had happened, though no one had told me directly. I must have pieced it together from different sources, conversations I'd overheard, my mother or father describing the event to others: a horse, a road, a car passing. When people pointed to the photograph and asked me who it was, I said it was my brother, Thomas, and that I never knew him, he died two years before I was born. I didn't understand why they said they were sorry. I knew it was a loss, but I couldn't feel it as one. He was a presence to me, not something taken away.

o

I played in a room at the east end of the house, the moat immediately outside. On clear mornings light bounced off the water through the windows, the white ceiling suddenly unstable with ripples and wind-stir, the surface of the moat reproduced in sunlight overhead. Our new freezer had just been delivered, and I'd got the cardboard box to customize into a secret house, a hatch cut into one side. My father was at work, dog-eared maps and his battered lunch tin on the passenger seat, and my mother was showing a group of history students round the house, so Patsy was here to keep an eye on me and Richard. I liked the threshold moments of crawling into or out of the den, the clement burrow darkness inside the box, the smell of cardboard, the enticing privacy and warmth. Lying on my back I could look through a crack in the roof and watch the ceiling's imitation of water.

Patsy tried to interest Richard in a book but he was restless, brooding, pacing the room. He noticed a pair of moorhens paddling close to the window and shouted at them – 'Shoo!' – as if they'd insulted him, and that eruption seemed to nudge the whole morning off its rails, because Rich stood there with both arms held out like a scarecrow's, his eyes half-closed, lids fluttering, as if there were static electricity in his eyelashes that made them flicker in and out of each other. His arms began to jerk; he turned round on the spot with his arms held out, jolting; the room went sludgy, as if a spell had swung us out of orbit and everything was slowing down – as if Patsy and I existed in our own current of time and were moving past Richard on a raft, keeping our eyes fixed on him. The spell lasted less than twenty seconds, and as he came through it he lowered his arms to his sides and saw both of us looking intently at him.

'What?' he said.

o

I was four when a local school performed *Twelfth Night* in our garden. A tiered, covered stand went up on the back lawn opposite the yew tree; stagehands rigged up lights and jammed the door on a writhe of power cables. The moat that ran along two sides of the lawn was now the sea around Illyria. Actors emerged from the water and dragged themselves onto dry land after the shipwreck. A spotlight picked out Feste standing on the flat roof above the bathroom on the east stairs. Malvolio's prison was a wooden cage fitted precisely to my square sandpit.

The drawing room's French windows opened onto an iron balcony where my father hung the bird-feeders. The stone that anchored the balcony was crumbling and we all knew better than to trust our weight to it. The play started after my bedtime, but the July nights were hot and my parents had left the windows open: I could hear the actors' voices, the audience laughing at mix-ups and pretensions; I slipped out of bed and crept across the landing, edging on all fours into the windows to watch through the ironwork.

The following summer the Banbury Cross Players performed *A Midsummer Night's Dream*. Each night I lay awake listening to the applause as Bottom and his crew approached in the punt and disembarked by the young copper beech in the corner. I couldn't sleep. I crawled across the landing and up the two carpeted steps to take my place at the balcony, a full moon spinning up like a cue-ball as Oberon and Titania summoned spirits from the shadows.

8

The rustic players reappeared in the punt, Peter Quince holding a lantern at the prow.

I was walking across that lawn with my mother when Dad appeared in the open windows and called out to us, 'Hold on one second.'

'Why?' I said.

'Keep your eyes on the window.'

He vanished. Mum and I watched the dark gap in the wall. Nothing happened, and I didn't understand why my father had made us stop, but then a blackbird shot from the side of the house, Dad appearing behind it, smiling, his arms spread like an impresario's, as if he'd just conjured the bird into existence.

A white china owl sat on a table next to the windows, the first thing I looked for when I pushed through the door from the landing. I came up the spiral staircase calling for my mother and father. I could hear voices. I went straight in, ready for the white owl. Richard was lying on the rug, on his back, his head close to the windows. My mother was kneeling beside him; my father stood next to her, leaning over. I stopped in the doorway. Richard wasn't moving. He lay rigid, his feet pointing up at the ceiling, his arms stretched along his sides, fists clenched.

'It's all right,' Dad said. 'Rich is having a fit. It's all right. It goes very quickly.'

Now he was shaking, his whole body thrumming. His arms bent at the elbows and straightened in stiff jerks, again and again; his knees rose off the floor and slammed down as his legs bent and extended; his feet kicked and stamped in repeated spasms. Dad had grabbed the cushion from his armchair, and Richard's head thudded into it, his teeth chomping together with a sound like horseshoes on tarmac.

'It's all right,' Mum said. 'We'll just wait for it to pass.'

I didn't move from the doorway. I watched my brother, the different parts of his body pounding the floor. The boards shook beneath him; vases and bowls vibrated on the tabletops; the French windows trembled in their frames.

o

Quartets, singers, harpsichordists and other musicians came to give charity concerts in the Great Hall. We pulled a dirty blue-grey cover across the carpet and used old rugs to dress the makeshift plank stage that lived in the garage. There were stacks of chairs in the stables loft and I watched teams of strangers deploy them in concentric arcs across the Great Hall, enthralled by event logistics and the anticipation that built through the afternoon. The room was new and strange with two hundred people in it and performers elegant in evening dress beneath suits of Spanish armour posed like sentries in the west wall niches; Mum led me in my dressing gown along the Groined Passage and we stood at the back through suites and sonatas.

I grew used to such invasions. I recognized the hubbub pitch of concert audiences and the python-thick cables of film-set lights. Film and TV crews moved in like desert caravans, grey production trucks inching through the gatehouse, the car park a camp of Winnebagos, Portakabins, catering vans and double-decker buses furnished with dining tables. Brawny carpenters and electricians smoked on the front lawn, bellies hanging over utility belts stocked with enviable commando inventories of tools, walkie-talkies and gaffer-tape reels; sparks fixed massive lights outside the windows and flooded interiors with unearthly platinum glare. I spent whole days wandering once-familiar rooms that set-dressers had skewed to their own purposes; I snapped the clapperboard and perched by the camera on the counter-weighted dolly crane; my mother apologized to assistant directors in navy Puffa jackets and we looked on quietly from the sidelines. We opened the gift shop in the stables and I sold Ian McKellen a postcard; I ran through the arch into the walled Ladies' Garden and saw Jane Seymour in a white Regency gown bend to sniff a rose; I was five when Morecambe and Wise came to shoot their Christmas show and I'd been in bed with flu all week, but my mother carried me downstairs so I could see the Great Hall garbed in vaudeville finery, Eric Morecambe walking over to greet me, adjusting his spectacles and barking, 'Hello! Are you married?'

Women in beauty spots and creamy pompadour wigs glide across the stone floor; Richard Chamberlain as Prince Charming kneels to fit the twinkling slipper; a stuntman in plumed tricorne hat and breeches leaps off the gatehouse onto a crashpad of cardboard boxes and foam. The rooms smell of dry ice and Elnett hairspray; extras dressed as monks eat corn flakes at the Dining Room table; Oliver Cromwell's warts are Rice Krispies painted brown and glued to his cheek and nose; the moat's deemed too placid to pass for the Thames so big pipes gush out of shot to ruffle the surface as Henry VIII's royal barge steers into view. One morning I found twenty human skeletons gathered on the lawn, each hanging by the skull from a slender metal stand so it appeared to be standing upright, the skeletons clustered in small groups as if I'd come across them at a garden party. Then actual men arrived and picked up the skeletons one by one, carrying them under their arms into the Great Hall like their own inner structures. These invasions brought the allure of make-believe and fired a boy's delight in gadgets and hardware, as if the camera tracks, cranes and trolleys, the hydraulic platforms that slid up and down the backs of prop vans, the walkie-talkies and grey-sleeved sound booms were versions of Scalextric, Meccano and Action Man equipment I'd yet to have the pleasure of. I climbed onto the deep window ledges in the Great Hall and crouched behind eighteenth-century leather fire buckets to watch swordfights from *Joseph Andrews* and *The Scarlet Pimpernel*, the actors in loose white shirts and gold-buckled shoes surging back and forth like dancers across the bare stone floor. They spent hours on the same sequence and I learned all the moves of the routine, the feints, parries, lunges, narrow escapes and exchanges of advantage, each time willing the less-gifted swordsman to buck his fate and fight back with a rage the choreographer had never sanctioned. Sometimes my attention drifted, the swordplay a backdrop of percussive cutlass sounds until the blades struck sparks off each other and I was gripped again.

Usually there were Civil War pikes, halberds and spontoons in here; a black cast-iron doorstop shaped like an elephant; huge logs heaped in the fireplace with bellows, andirons and Victorian copper bedpans leaning on either side; and a gamut of swords – Mameluke short swords, Pappenheimer rapiers, plain and basket-hilt broadswords – fixed to the bare stone walls. In January 1938, the Trustees of the Natural History Museum in London had directed the keepers of departments to consider how to protect their collections in the event of aerial attack. The keepers drew up lists of specimens and documents to be evacuated in case of war, and by the beginning of the bombing of London in August 1940 the Great Hall had become a warehouse for fifty-four green and white super-cabinets of mammals, thirty-eight boxes of mollusca and six hundred and sixty-two bundles of books and papers (arranged in pressmark order, so they could be referred to if necessary) stacked one on top of the other, among them the stuffed or mounted skins of lion, snow leopard, spotted hyena, polar bear, wolf, sea lion, bushpig, Weddell seal, wallaby and pygmy hog.

So I walked across the room imagining crates stacked to the ceiling, animals coming alive at night and forcing the lids. I learned to ride a bicycle in the Great Hall. My mother wiped down the wheels on the carpet's behalf and I rode circles round refectory tables and crimson plush sofas, off the wool kerb onto smooth flagstones, while Mum used WD40 to condition suits of armour and visored helmets called burgonets, and rubbed beeswax polish into the oak shoulders of blunderbusses and muskets displayed among the swords.

For my parents those film-crew days were a mixed blessing. The house needed the money but they watched anxiously as strangers lugged sharp-cornered gear through medieval doorways and leaned spiky lighting rigs against Tudor panelling. Dad haunts the sets like the house's guardian spirit, vigilant for carelessness. It's as if his nervous system spreads through the whole building, so that a slammed door or a pewter bowl set down too briskly hurts him as keenly as a cut on the arm. He's up at dawn to turn the alarm off and slide the bolts on the oak outer door (the slide and rich bass clonk of the bolts roll round the acoustic chamber of the porch); ducks waddle behind him across the front lawn and loiter by the stables while he scoops a wooden dish through the grain bin; he scatters grain for ducks like a man in an old Dutch painting. At night he or my mother go round the house checking doors and windows, turning lights off. They call it 'shutting the house up' – a daily task with its own ceremonial rhythm, an established itinerary followed from one room to another. The remote, formal spaces of the house are eerie in the dark. The grandfather clock ticks implacably down the Long Gallery; floorboards creak like ships' hulls under pressure from the swell; there's a sudden breath of cold wind from stone spiral stairs; the men and women in portraits have occult power in the moonlight through high windows. I'm used to the ten or fifteen minutes each evening when either my mother or father disappears into the other end. They open the door in the music room and step into historical dark. We're all still in the same house, but for that short interval they're away, the plain door a portal or time machine by which you passed into a different world. The minutes stretch out in our lamp-lit domestic realm while my father goes off into that elsewhere. At last the door by the piano clicks open and he joins us again in the kitchen, the cold in his clothes a trace of that other region like moondust on an astronaut.

Sometimes I went with them. I followed them through the Great Hall, down the Long Gallery, into the Kings' Chamber, Council Chamber, Queen Anne's Room, Great Parlour and Chapel. Wooden shutters unfold from the walls; the Great Parlour's huge blue blinds pull down like square-rigged sails on the west windows; you have to reach behind an iron breastplate to switch off the light in the Groined Passage. I hardly ever went there alone after dark. The eyes in portraits followed me down the gallery; white busts of Ben Jonson and Inigo Jones began to shoulder off their plinths; oak chests were dark blocks the size of tombs and the pendants in the Great Hall's plaster ceiling were ready to detach and plummet just as you walked beneath them. But it's in the dark that you register most vividly each room's distinctive climate and smell: the Dining Room and Groined Passage and the stairs up to the Chapel have bare stone floors and vaulted ceilings and there's a cave-like chill and clean, mineral air to these unadorned medieval spaces; the Oak Room feels warmer by several degrees and smells of wood and wool; the rush matting of the Kings' Chamber (which my mother waters like a lawn, swinging the can from side to side) turns the room into a humid, semi-tropical biome in which the twining plants, butterflies and birds on the eighteenth-century Chinese wallpaper are entirely at home.

o

For a long time it was assumed that seizures were incited by supernatural forces. They were sent by gods, or caused by demons entering the patient. The violent attacks were thought to be punishments for sins committed by the sufferer or by his parents against gods, particularly against Selene, goddess of the moon. The ancient Greeks called epilepsy 'the sacred disease'. A seizure was a bad omen, and a person with epilepsy was an object of horror and disgust: anyone who touched him might themselves be possessed; by spitting, you could keep the demon at bay and avoid infection.

Since the disease was understood to be an infliction or possession by a god, demon or ghost, its cure was also assumed to be supernatural. An iron nail hammered where the sufferer had first laid his head would pin the evil spirit to the spot. Magicians forbade patients from taking baths, from wearing black garments or goat skins, from crossing their feet or hands, and from eating red mullet, eel, goat, deer, mint, garlic and onions. Recommended treatments included seal genitals, tortoise blood and hippopotamus testicles, and peony root worn round the neck on an amulet. Pliny records the sight of people with epilepsy drinking the blood of wounded gladiators in the arena.

The word 'epilepsy' comes from the Greek verb *epilambanein*, which means 'to seize'. So epilepsy is the illness of being seized: a condition characterized by recurrent seizures. The author of *On the Sacred Disease*, part of the Hippocratic collection of medical texts from around 400 BC, rejected the orthodox view that epilepsy was incited by supernatural agencies. 'It has a natural cause just as other diseases have,' he wrote. 'Men think it is divine merely because they do not understand it.' Seizures, he argued, were not caused by higher powers, but by an abnormality in the brain; they were triggered by 'change of winds and of temperature, and, in children, fright and fear,' and should be treated with drugs and diet, not magic.

Richard had had an ear infection when he was two and a half. At night, provoked by high fever, he'd started to convulse. Doctors told my parents these febrile convulsions weren't uncommon among children, and that in most cases they passed without further complications. But Richard began to have other kinds of seizures. His head dropped as if a hinge in his neck had suddenly loosened, his arms lifting at full stretch in front of him, these salaam attacks coming so frequently that a bump developed on his forehead where he'd slammed into the edges of tables and basins: at breakfast, Mum sat beside him with her arm stretched out, her hand on the table edge to cushion the blow. Atonic or drop attacks felled him without warning, as if all his bone-strength had deserted him on a whim. Absence seizures stole his awareness for a few seconds, Rich staring blankly, eyelids fluttering, his head dropping before he looked up and carried on eating or talking as if nothing had happened. Sometimes his arm flew up as if he'd touched a red-hot coal: he was holding a glass when one of these myoclonic jerks raced through him; the glass shot from his hand and smashed on the ceiling in a squall of crystals and water. At three, he'd begun to have tonic-clonic seizures in which he lost consciousness and fell, his whole body stiffening in the tonic phase before the clonic phase of uncontrolled, spasmodic jerking. Antiepileptic drugs like phenobarbitone left him sluggish, his speech drawn out and laboured, as if all the machinery of his intelligence had slowed down.

The seizures often came at night. Martin or Susannah walked through the dressing room in the half-dark to tell our parents Rich was having a fit. My mother and father went up and down the narrow stone stairs to his bedroom to check on him in the aftermath. He'd fall into deep sleep, as if each attack had been a test of physical and mental endurance. These full-blown night seizures left him shaken, his speech low and slurred, one word dissolving into another, and the next day he'd move cautiously, as if he'd just returned to the world after long absence and couldn't trust the fundamental laws. When we sat down for lunch, he stared blankly at the table. Mum looked at him, wondering if he was having an absence seizure. Rich straightened suddenly, as if emerging from a trance.

'Sorry?' he asked.

No one had said anything.

It was as if he were passing in and out of some other realm none of us had any picture of.

A teacher rang to say he'd had a bad attack, different from the others. It had started like a typical tonic-clonic, his body stiffening before the violent, jerking spasms began, his arms, legs and head beating on the floor. She'd slipped a cushion below his head and knelt beside him, waiting for the seizure to pass. Usually, after the clonic phase, Richard's muscles would relax, his body would settle back into itself, unconscious, his chest rising and falling with deep, noisy breaths. But this time when the spasms dwindled his body stiffened again, and then his limbs started to jerk once more, as if he'd passed from one seizure into another without any period of recovery in between. The seizures weren't stopping. An ambulance had taken him to hospital. He was in Intensive Care. Doctors used a term none of us had heard before: *Status epilepticus.*

o

Sometimes I looked out in the morning to find ten or twelve men sitting on folding stools beneath broad green umbrellas round the far side of the moat. Angling clubs got started at dawn: they might have emerged from the ground overnight, a dozen mounds of waterproofs and tackle boxes, fishermen ranged round the bank like numbers on a clock, each encampment supplied with thermos flasks and air-tight containers, bags of groundbait, old margarine tubs crawling with maggots, keepnets like green mesh tunnels down into the water. When you opened a tackle box the multi-storey trays separated themselves outwards to reveal weights, hooks, floats, lures and reels in neat compartments. I'd run out first thing, crossing the bridge to visit the fish-ermen, enthralled by technical gear and angling jargon I was just getting the hang of. Some of the men resisted any intrusion into their solitude, the quiet umbrella world they'd made and got ensconced in; others were quick to draw up their keepnet so I could see the writhe and glisten of perch, roach and tench in the closed end.

I got my first fishing rod for Christmas when I was five and pressed wodges of white bread round hooks to dangle among minnows in the warmer water against the bridge, tiny elastic bands holding the line against the float. From the bridge I could see minnows nosing the bread; I could see the bread already disintegrating in the water; otherwise the surface was unfathomable and you had to trust the float to describe by bobs and twitches the action down below. I learned to strike when I felt the right weight and tremor in the rod, but I didn't like the gory business of working the barbed hook out while the perch with its spiky dorsals threshed under my hand. I graduated to a longer rod with a cork butt and black-finished spinning reel, and dumped the floats for a selection of silver lures with red and black fish-eyes and scale details painted on them. These spinners had double or triple hooks and were designed for pike.

I walked round the moat again and again in search of pike. When it was hot, they liked to bask in the shallows, and if you were lucky you'd come across one hanging close to the bank, two feet long, a mean platypus flatness at the nose, motionless except for slight featherings of side fins to maintain position, its shadow a distinct bar on the mud bottom. I froze when I found a pike. If I got any closer or even just lifted my hand slightly the fish would startle and vanish in a precise turbulence like a muscle spasm in the water. Sometimes it knew I was there, and I knew one more movement would trigger the violent disappearance: I was involved in a small, local suspense in which everything but the pike and my nearness to it was peripheral, held in abeyance. I tried not to breathe.

You could control the level of the moat by cranking the sluice gate in the south-east corner: with the gate up, the moat joined the Sor Brook just before it dropped off the waterfall by Harry Bennett's. When the moat was low you'd get a band of rough, muddy beach strewn with white stones, potsherds, algae piles and sheep bones, a wrack-stench of vegetation rotting down, and I'd work my way along like a beachcomber, picking up pieces of china and medieval iron implements, the neck of an old clay bottle with relief decorations around it, bases of stoneware jugs, hieroglyph prints of herons' feet in the mud.

Dad let the moat down like this so the fish man Richard Morgan could trawl for stock. He arrived in a pick-up truck with white polystyrene crates in the back, and soon three or four men in drysuits were dragging a buoyed net through chest-high water, filling buckets with fingerlings. Sometimes they used electrodes to send a shock through the water, and we'd stand around watching stunned fish rise to the surface like souls of the dead. Most of all I wanted to hear Richard Morgan talk about pike. I imagined huge, ancient specimens flushed from secret depths, the moat's version of sharks, predators in its dark places. Perch, roach and tench were just fish, but pike were touched with violence and death.

So the stakes were higher when I went out with my new rod rigged with a spinner. The lure's weight carried the line wherever you wanted; the reel made a low clunk as the mechanism engaged; when you reeled in, the lure appeared again in brown-green shallows. Soon there was a rhythm to this, the faint breath sound of line frisking through the eyelets, the far plop of the lure, the clunk of the reel's gear locking into place, the dripping from the lure as you lifted it out and back to throw the cast again – a rhythm that made the first strike even more of a surprise, the rod suddenly bending to the tension, tremulous concentric ripples spreading where the taut line entered the water, my hands alive with a struggling, muscular weight, unmistakably pike. No skill involved, you just kept reeling in, until the pike was threshing on the surface, and then on the grass, head and tail thwacking the ground. I didn't know what to do; I had no idea how to kill a pike; I was thrilled and frightened by the size of the fish, the long, flat jaw crammed with angled-back teeth; I carried the whole thing inside, pike dangling from the rod, and called out for my mother and father. No one answered, so I carried the fish upstairs and backed into the drawing room. Mum looked up from her desk and saw me with the fishing rod, the pike still twitching, fish water dripping off it onto the rug in front of the French windows.

'I caught a pike,' I said.

o

The *Status epilepticus* had scarred Richard's brain. A neurologist reported brain damage: 'cerebral atrophy in the frontal lobes'. The first institution was a red-brick Victorian hospital near Reading which I saw in glimpses when Mum took me to collect Rich for a weekend or holiday: male nurses in two-piece white uniforms; vast iron radiators in linoleum-floored corridors; wire grilles reinforcing the window glass; the day-room TV tuned to the snooker. The hospital smelled of catering, dirty clothes and disinfectant; some of the residents wore plastic helmets buckled under the chin to protect their heads when seizures felled them; everyone wore slippers – hard shoes caused too many injuries when fights broke out.

Later, he'd come home by train and we'd pick him up from the station, Rich last on the platform, his blue and yellow Leeds United holdall stuffed to bursting, touch and go if the zip would hold. He'd supported Leeds since they won the championship in 1969, unbeaten at home all season, and when they won it again in 1974 he'd hung on the result of every game and had the whole team by heart, names I learned just by hearing my brother repeat them so often: Billy Bremner, Mick Jones, Allan Clarke, Joe Jordan, Gordon McQueen. Along with the Leeds holdall he'd have a plastic bag with that week's issue of *Shoot!* or *Match* magazine in it, plus a *Sun* or *Daily Star*, Rich showing off the topless girls with a lewdness borrowed from other residents at the centre, his magazines rolled into neat pipes like runners' batons, the same exacting thoroughness applied to rolling a magazine as he'd bring to filling the Leeds holdall, kneeling beside it after packing, pressing down repeatedly with straight arms as if he was giving it cardiac massage, then using brute force to haul the zip.

The return home was sunlit, ascendant time. Here were stickers of Leeds United players in dependable formation on his bedroom door, the Leeds United rug Dad called 'the prayer mat' beside his bed, the poster of a heron among reeds, the two carved herons on the windowsill with their heads back and beaks pointing straight up like spires. We both loved herons. There was a heron nest in a fork of oak branches behind the kitchen gardens, big enough for a boy to sleep in; when I saw a heron fly past over the water I thought of pterodactyls in my dinosaur book and the film of Conan Doyle's *The Lost World* – a prehistoric aspect to the pleated neck and slow, heavy wingbeats. Rich was vigilant for herons and stalked the moat in search of them. He took my father's binoculars in the leather case with varicoloured racecourse tags tied to the shoulder strap and walked the banks until he glimpsed the bird's angular pose on the far side of the water. Once, as the car crossed the bridge, bringing him home again, he said he loved the *heronity* of the moat, and this new coinage fired something in him: he smiled, and kept repeating it, savouring the word, turning it over: *heronity, heronity, heronity*.

Those hours Rich spent watching herons were a state of grace from which he returned restored and at peace, but often these visits home were fraught with difficulty. The seizures kept coming, an average of five full-blown tonic-clonic attacks every month, and on top of these he was showing cognitive and behavioural problems associated with frontal-lobe damage: lack of initiative, insight, flexibility and self-control; failure to see other points of view. Sedated by anti-convulsants, he sleeps in till two o'clock and comes downstairs in his dressing gown, the cord drawn tight round his tummy; he wears a T-shirt and pants and socks under his pyjamas. He opens the fridge and scans the shelves with a blank, drugged gaze; he eats in front of the TV upstairs, the circuits of a Grand Prix a kind of mesmerism he can't shift his gaze from. My mother and father try to nudge him out of this stupor; they try to persuade him to wash, or get dressed and go outside, but he keeps his eyes on the droning cars and says, 'I'm busy,' or, 'Watch your

mouth,' or, 'Don't speak till you're spoken to,' the air prick-
ling with menace. He picks up these expressions from the
red-brick Victorian asylum – 'You and whose army?'; 'You
better wash your mouth out with soap'; 'Shut your face,
or I'll shut it for you' – and tries them out on us, charged
by the force of the words as he repeats them to himself, the
violence implicit in his language reinforced by his physical
presence, a wild, unpredictable power winding itself tighter
inside his chest, his bolshy expressions preliminary fumarole
spurts before the volcano blows. He makes a fist and holds
it to Dad's chin, posing the impact. Mum's left a heavy black
cast-iron frying pan on the left-hand hob, hottest of the
two, and in a rush of terrible inspiration Rich grabs it and
holds the flat bottom against her cheek like a branding iron:
she wears a headscarf on the school run next morning to
hide the burn. Sunday afternoon comes round, time for
the drive back to Reading, but Rich refuses to go. He comes
out of the kitchen with the kitchen scissors and bends to the
corners to cut the telephone wires. He yanks the car keys
from the ignition and flings them in the moat. He holds the
scissors out in front of him, stabbing them like a dagger at
anyone who approaches. My sister runs to fetch Bert
Dancer, and Bert wrestles Richard down onto the bed in the
playroom and lies on top of him. I saw them through
the doorway, my brother's fists beating on the older man's
back, his legs kicking.

Once, at bathtime, Mum locked the two of us in the
downstairs bathroom. Rich was marauding through the

house, a poltergeist spinning through rooms, Dad trying to calm him down. I dribbled Captain Pugwash bubble-bath under the taps and my mother sat on the cork-topped seat beside the bath with her hands clasped in her lap, looking at the floor. The ceiling bulb was covered with a bowl of smoked white glass and you could see the shapes of dead flies in it. Now Rich was in the playroom outside and he was yelling through the thin door, shouting at my mother to open it. I know he's put his shoulder to it because the whole thing warps inwards off the bolt, and then the bathroom fills with a series of splintery booms as he kicks in the bottom plywood panels. One of these impacts sends a shudder up through the wall that shakes the smoked glass bowl off its clips and it drops straight down onto the grey tiles, exploding with a crash of shrapnel against the side of the bath and the toilet pedestal. There's silence, the explosion a kind of shock treatment that jars Rich out of his frenzy; now we just have to keep our distance and wait for the storm to pass. Harry Bennett came in his sun-faded navy overalls and repaired the door with a rectangle of new plywood, the outline visible through two coats of white gloss like a plaque fixed in memory of the episode.

o

The first form of biological electricity to receive attention from scientists was that found in various species of electric fish, especially the electric eel, Nile catfish and Mediterranean torpedo. These fish can transmit an electric shock.

Aristotle, Pliny and Galen all described the power of torpedoes to produce a numbing sensation when touched. The Roman physician Scribonius Largus recorded the use of electric fish as a remedy for headaches, recommending a live black torpedo placed on whichever part of the head was in pain until the patient felt the numbness following shock. Others recommended torpedo shocks as a cure for gout: patients should stand barefoot on the fish until its power weakened.

Devices for producing electricity began to appear in the eighteenth century. Johann Winkler, a professor in Leipzig, could charge himself from a 'friction machine' and set glasses of brandy on fire by throwing sparks from his tongue. A device for storing electricity was invented in 1745 by Ewald von Kleist, dean of the cathedral at Carmin, in northern Germany, and also independently the following year by Pieter van Musschenbroek, a physicist at the University of Leyden, in Holland. This primitive battery, called a 'Leyden jar' by Abbé Jean Antoine Nollet, allowed physicists to store and transport electricity, and provided a source of transient electric currents. Abbé Nollet, 'experimenter' to Louis XV, discharged a Leyden jar through a hundred and eighty royal guards in front of the King in the Grande Gallerie at Versailles, and then through the entire membership of a Carthusian monastery, who held hands in a line and all jumped at the same time as the shock hurtled through them.

Between 1749 and 1753, the French naturalist Michel

Adanson studied the Nile catfish, *Malapterus electricus*, in Senegal, and compared its shock to that produced by a Leyden jar. In 1769, Edward Bancroft, an American physician living in Surinam, described a series of experiments he'd conducted on electric eels, *Gymnotus electricus*, showing that the fish's shock was transmitted by water and could travel in a wave through a line of people holding hands.

In 1772, inspired by Bancroft, John Walsh began to study torpedoes caught off the French coast near La Rochelle. Assisted by his nephew, Arthur, Walsh obtained his first specimen on June 30th. 'She gave us a both a shock,' he reported; 'both instantaneous in the commencement, and ending; precisely like the Electric shock!' Like Adanson, Walsh found the shock he received from the fish identical to that transmitted by a Leyden jar. 'On this my first experiment on the effect of the Torpedo,' he wrote, 'I exclaimed this is certainly Electricity – but how?' After further experiments, Walsh reported that the torpedo could discharge fifty or more shocks in a minute and a half, and that the fish's electricity could be transmitted through wires attached to its upper and lower surfaces. In 1775, he showed that a discharge from an electric eel could produce a spark capable of jumping across a small gap in tinfoil. Henry Cavendish, who developed Walsh's work on torpedoes, concluded that there was 'nothing in the phenomena of the torpedo at all incompatible with electricity.'

o

Most of the time Richard was away at the epilepsy centre and the twins were away at boarding school. Left to my own devices, I had the free run of the house and garden. Bert fixed a blue nylon rope ladder, a swing and a straw-coloured rope with three knots in it to the lowest branch of the copper beech that leaned over the moat at a Pisa angle by the stables. In April and May the young leaves were translucent and looked like the skins of red grapes stretched on fish bones. The lower branches hung down until their tips were almost touching the ground, ropes dangling inside a skirt of leaves. In war films I'd seen how you scaled a rope ladder from the side, heels on the rungs, and once I'd mastered this I spent hours working my way up the knotted rope, aiming for the bough. I sat facing the moat on the swing, straightening my legs and folding them tight under me, extending the arc until I was swinging right up into the leaves, relishing the weightless hiatus moment between upswing and downswing, poised among branches, imagining that if I timed it right and let go as the swing rushed me upwards I'd have momentum to burst through the canopy and soar over the water, in flight for a few seconds before splashdown.

In 1900 the castle had employed fourteen gardeners. The house had been draped in ivy, the west lawn home to a vast sundial of clipped yew. On the far side of the moat a well-tended path had run between the water and a profusion of shrubs and roses, and wherever you looked there had been topiary novelties and labour-intensive beds of bright-coloured annuals. The kitchen gardens beyond the church, enclosed in high walls of heat-retaining pink brick, had once sported rhubarb bells, forcing beds for pineapples, glasshouses for tomatoes and cucumbers, tangles of runner beans along strings, drills of carrots, potatoes, cabbages and lettuces, and fruit trees spread-eagled in espaliers, Mrs Green's husband Charlie Green using a rabbit's tail attached to a stick to pollinate the peach blossoms.

Dad turned the kitchen gardens over to the village for use as allotments: I knew a place the size of a football field portioned into rectangular plots where men I recognized from church and open days leaned companionably on spades. Often I crossed the bridge over the brook and pushed through the iron gates into the kitchen gardens. I haunted the long, low Victorian greenhouse with broken panes, wasps crawling the windfall from apple trees, cobwebs sagging off the roofwork, a debris of smashed pots and a narrow brick walkway between rotten, mossed-over workbenches, rich plant gas coming off the nettle clumps. I kept going back to the ruined greenhouse but I had to dare myself to approach the musty half-underground darkness of the boiler room at the far end, tiptoeing from brick to brick along the aisle, breathing humid, tropical air. I wanted to reach the far end without stepping on a crack; looking ahead, I could just make out the wrecked boiler among nettles and dangling ivy, a steamboat abandoned in jungle.

My parents kept on one gardener. Bert Dancer had a big mole on his chin; his hair was dark tarnished silver, precisely combed; he wore grey wool trousers, black work boots with protective toecaps, and a sleeveless V-necked sweater, shirt-sleeves rolled up on tanned forearms. He had a full set of false teeth he could detach and push out on his tongue, as if his grin were playing truant from his other features. Bert sat on the roller-seat behind the green Dennis lawnmower with its curved front-mounted bin. To turn the Dennis round you had to swing it in a wide circle, the moulded steel seat on top of the roller banking and lifting before you got set on a straight course again. There were lawns on the north, west and south sides of the house and Bert mowed them in lovely pinafore stripes of lighter and darker green; the bin filled with cut grass that Bert tipped onto an old sheet, and when the heap was three or four bins high he'd gather the corners together and heave the rounded white sack onto his shoulders, carrying it like Atlas under the gatehouse, across the moat, past the church to the car park overseen by Juno – her massive white head on a mica-specked granite plinth. The mound of cut grass grew all summer: I pushed my arm into it, up to the shoulder, feeling the heat generated by grass already decomposing in the core.

I rode the Dennis too, standing on the roller platform or sharing the moulded seat with Bert as he worked the brakes and gears and pushed the long handlebar away to swing the turns. We mowed right to the edge of the moat and swung back to face the house again, white specks of daisies in among the green clippings. I wasn't on board when Bert lost control and the Dennis got away from him, sliding off the bank into the moat. The mower and roller seat were completely engulfed, but Bert had jumped off like a pilot ejecting just before the machine hit the water. It took a tractor to drag it out, Mr Dancer standing chest-deep in the moat to fix ropes, planks laid in at angles to make a slipway – a salvage job, water pouring off the Dennis as it made dry land again to cheers and applause, dripping ropes drawn taut like piano strings.

Bored of the swing and rope ladder, I'd cross the bridge and climb the old horse chestnut by the churchyard railings. The chestnut had been a pollard: its branches grew from a low stool you could sit in, a woody throne room with a mulch of rainwater and leaf mould underfoot, tree structure rising on all sides, light screened off by wet chestnut leaves. Further round the moat, a holly tree stood alongside a tall oak. If you pushed through the holly's prickly outer layer you could use the branches as a ladder up the oak, and if you climbed right to the top you could drag yourself onto the lowest oak branch where Harry Bennett had knocked up a rudimentary tree-shack from old planks and plywood offcuts, a hutch of nest-like privacy and snugness, an owl's perch for keeping tabs on herons or eavesdropping on coot and moorhen business down below.

I kept going round the moat, ducking through bushes and trees to the sluice gate in the corner, a rusty toothed crankshaft poking up, an exotic region of bamboo and ele-phant rhubarb beyond it, a lost green world I sometimes rowed over to, checking from far-off for kingfishers in the ash bough that hung over the sluice. Water flowed in and out through the gate, the corner crowded with moat-scum, a rank flotsam of duck turds and rotting leaves, the furred stems and wrinkled dark foliage of the elephant rhubarb complicit with decay. To see the muscle spasm of a pike's disappearance here in the rotten murk was to get close to the moat's underbelly and usually I kept my distance, rowing out instead along the open straights.

Our boat was a military green of hard heavy plastic and catamaran design. I fetched rowlocks and splintery oars from the Old Kitchens, a warren of pitch-dark rooms that had the right subterranean clamminess and cobweb dangle to pass for dungeons. This summer the moat's infested by a pale green algae, the water invisible beneath a thick, gassy cover that's like a continuously effervescing eiderdown. The algae seems alive with animal rather than vegetable person-ality and it's so invasive and self-multiplying that at night I imagine it spreading inwards over the banks and lawns until it's tented the whole house in green, gelid light. Rich is here, Dad's come home with a sack of algicide, and the three of us push the boat out into this limbo medium that's neither land nor water. Rowing's exhausting, the blades coming up draped with weed, and Rich and I take turns while Dad sits at the back next to the wood square you'd fix an outboard to and opens up the bag of poison. I'm still small and have to use Dad's feet as footrests when I row, and with each pull of the oars I can feel the effort passing through my feet into his, and when Rich rows I sit at the prow watching the gunk pass sluggishly beneath us. I don't have to see my brother's face to know his tongue will be pushing inside his cheek while he bends his full concentration to the oars and Dad comments like a coxswain, 'That's right, Rich. Just a bit further. Let's get over to that corner. That's it.' So piece by piece we work our way along, Dad using his hand to scoop through the sack and scatter gritty meal across the green; we're doing all this in silence now and the task has devotional measure and progress, Dad's hand moving from side to side with fingers open as if he were sowing seed in a field or scattering someone's ashes in a place they'd loved above all others. Water lilies could also get out of hand but it was no good grabbing the greasy cords and trying to yank them up while dragonflies lorded it over the pads.

o

The castle was open to the public three afternoons a week from Easter to September. Mrs May ran a tea room in the stables. She bred shi-tzus and wore large photosensitive glasses that turned caramel-brown as soon as she stepped outside; she had ice creams delivered twice a year and I leaned over the chest freezer to check the brands. People spilled onto the front lawn by the beech sapling that was the same age as me and poured tea from clinky steel pots and ate scones, and sometimes Rich lingered among them, starting conversations, letting it slip that actually he lives here and, well, he probably won't have a cup of tea, he'll make himself a coffee in the kitchen, in his Leeds mug, and then he'll come out again holding the mug in both hands like a chalice, slurping coffee off the brim, and make sure everyone sees the Leeds crest, holding it up close to their faces, saying, 'That's right. I'm *proud* to be a Leeds supporter!'

A crow staked out territory on the lawn and waited for crumbs. Gaining confidence, it lurched into the porch and knocked with its beak on the door glass. One afternoon I saw the crow approach a man lying on his back smoking a cigarette. The crow was standing about a yard from his head when the man turned his face and looked the bird straight in the eye. He took the cigarette from his mouth and offered it butt-end to the crow, which stretched its fat neck forward and took the cigarette in its beak and straightened, the man letting go at just the right moment, the crow smoking a cigarette under the beech tree. I broke into a run, impatient to tell anyone who'd listen what I'd just seen.

On these open days Dad sat at the folding outdoor table on the bridge, selling entry tickets and guidebooks to visitors wandering in past the church, and sometimes I sat beside him and thumbed the clickers to count adults and children coming through. In the mornings I tagged along behind my mother, her arms full of flowers for cut-glass vases in the Oak Room and Long Gallery. I lugged the watering can upstairs for sprinkling the rush matting in the Kings' Chamber, and clambered over Gallery radiators while Mum mixed red and yellow acrylic paints to match the original orange-pink of the wallpaper that was faded from sun-exposure and smirched with damp, and watched while she rubbed Pliantine preserver into leather-bound books like John Evelyn's *Silva* in the small library off the Great Hall. Impatient, I spun the faded yellow-green globe and ran my hands over ribbed leather spines, titles and authors in gilt lettering – Milton, Schiller, Pascal, Pope, Gibbon and Keats among them, but these books tiny and impotent amidst the massed ranks of nineteenth-century biblical commentaries, multi-volume editions of Froissart's *Chronicles*, Hutton's *Philosophy*, Watson's *Theological Tracts*, Baker's *Livy*, the sermons and lectures of Massillon, White, Boyle, Beveridge, Taylor and Waterland. Here were herbals and floras, military histories and biographies, a whole section devoted to Aristotle, Juvenal, Tacitus, Virgil, Homer, Lucretius, Herodotus, Catullus, Aeschylus, Sophocles and Cicero in the original Latin and Greek.

But I ignored all these. The book I kept returning to was one my father had pulled out and shown me, a scholarly monograph by a distant relative called Edward Twisleton, published in 1873. *The Tongue Not Essential to Speech* presented a series of case studies demonstrating that it was possible to speak intelligibly without a tongue. Huneric, King of the Vandals, tortured Catholics in fifth-century North Africa by amputating their tongues, yet still they were able to speak. In 1630, the French doctor Jacques Roland treated an eight-year-old boy who'd contracted smallpox and lost his tongue to gangrene; he too was able to speak. In 1652, a Dutchman known as Joannes the Dumb fell into the hands of Turkish pirates on a voyage to Italy: they cut out his tongue and he didn't talk for three years, until a flash of lightning at night prompted him to recover his voice. Twisleton wished to refute the idea that these were miracles, evidence of divine intervention. There were natural explanations for all these cases. You didn't need gods to help you speak without a tongue.

o

Joyce lived with her brother in one of the Victorian almshouses. She'd been coming to work at the house since 1943, when she was sixteen, first as parlour maid, later as cook; she walked down the hill each weekday morning in blue coat and headscarf, rocking from side to side. Mrs Upton walked from her cottage in the ironstone row beyond the almshouses, Bert and Mrs Dancer walked from their house overlooking the kitchen gardens, and Mrs Green arrived on her bicycle from Tadmarton, half-dismounting as she approached the castle, coasting the last stretch standing on one pedal, then stepping off nimbly and running alongside the bike as she brought it to a halt.

Mrs Green and Mrs Upton worked in tandem; they swept, dusted and polished the large cold rooms to the west through which visitors sauntered on Wednesday, Thursday and Sunday afternoons, rooms that were both part of my home and yet strange to me, formal and unfrequented, the other end. Mrs Green was slim, with cotton-white hair; Mrs Upton was shorter, stockier; her hair was wire-wool grey and she wore glasses. No one used their first names; I didn't even know if they had them. They wore blue smocks and knelt to rub O-Cedar oil into the oak stairs, and you could tell where Mrs Upton had been working because bits of string from her string mop got snagged on floorboard splinters.

Mid-morning, they came into the kitchen for coffee. I'd last seen them passing through the door into the public side: it seemed they lived in that other world of portraits, plaster ceilings, suits of armour, swords. In the corner, under domed wire-gauze fly-guards that hung on nails like fencing masks, Joyce sat on her high stool, feet on the rung. The kitchen was her domain. She put a pan of milk on the hob, a china puck sitting in the bottom to stop it boiling over, and made milky coffee for Mrs Upton, Mrs Green and Mrs Dancer, and hot chocolate for Bert, who arrived with the cut-grass smell on him, unhitching his dentures so his teeth floated out towards me on his tongue. By half-past ten they'd have gathered in the kitchen, Joyce perched on her stool like a tennis umpire, a bowl of cake mixture in her lap while Mrs Upton, Mrs Green, Bert and Mrs Dancer too sat round the green Formica table, delving into the Victoria biscuit tin, Joyce like a mother hen presiding over her chicks, providing for them.

If I weren't at school, I'd sit with them.

'How old do you think I am?' Mrs Dancer asked.

'I don't know.'

'I'm about the same age as my tongue and a little bit older than my teeth.'

She said the chewy black pieces in Garibaldi biscuits

were squashed flies, and looked to the others for corroboration. Mrs Upton was the most forthright in everything, talking as if language had been welling up in her overnight and this was the first opportunity for overspill.

'It's a nice day, isn't it? A nice day to be outside, I'd say. We don't get many of them, do we, so you've got to take advantage while you can. There's no telling what it'll be like tomorrow. I don't understand them people nowadays who just want to sit inside. Sometimes I think they don't know what they're missing. Sat inside watching the television all day all night, when you've only got to look out the window to see it's beautiful.'

The ladies who gathered in the kitchen each morning loved seeing Richard.

'Look out, here's trouble!' Mrs Dancer said.

'How are you, then, Richard?' Mrs Green asked.

'Very well thanks, Mrs Green,' Rich replied. 'All the better for seeing you!'

Joyce made him coffee in his Leeds United mug. He leaned over the hob, waiting for milk to billow up the sides of the pan. 'All the better for seeing you,' he repeated, half to himself, laughing. Joyce was peeling apples, and Rich turned to her and said, 'How's your little dog, Joyce?'

'Still the same, thank you, Richard. Full of devilry!'

Mrs Upton and Mrs Green were remembering Mrs French who used to live in the Toll Cottage on the main road, not so much a conversation as a monologue by Mrs Upton, Mrs Green an affirmative Chorus.

'She put that fence around it, Mrs French did. She liked to be shut in. She was a very *thorough* woman.'

'Oh, she was.'

'She used to polish her gates with furniture polish!'

'Oh, she did.'

'It used to have such loving care, with her.'

'She told me on the bus one day,' Mrs Green began, 'I was sat with her on the bus and she said, about people saying that she was always at work, she said, "That's the way I like it," she said. "And when I can't do it,' she said, "I hope I shall be taken." And she was, three weeks later.'

But the mention of gates has cleared a path in Mrs Upton's memory, and she hurries down it, leaving Mrs French behind.

'There used to be gates – do you remember? – special gates for people to carry their coffins over from North Newington. The gates were made specially to rest the coffins on. Now that's all gone.'

'Along the Chaddle?' Mrs Green asks.

'That's right, along the Chaddle. See, there were no way of getting them here. That's all gone now. It's a shame, really. Of course, I'm very much for the *old things*. It's like the stone stiles: they're all gone. Now the stiles are so high up it's a job for me to get over them, they've got those two stepping things, and there's one over by the sewer I nearly broke my back on – there's a ditch on the other side and I went right down into it! There used to be a stone one at the top of the park, but that's gone too. Everything's gone, really. All the medieval stuff that should belong to the castle, that's all gone. See what I mean? I'm very much for the old things.'

One morning we talk about ghosts. Mrs Upton and Mrs Green remember how they'd both seen, on separate occasions, the figure of a Puritan preacher walking across the bridge under the gatehouse, this man in a black buttoned gown and broad-brimmed black hat. It was early; they were walking towards the house, across the cattle grid by the church. There's a morning fog over the moat so you can hardly make out the bridge walls – just this man in curious dress, as if he's slipped out of history, moving in the fog, disappearing into the arch. Mrs Upton says she wouldn't have bothered about him if months later she hadn't heard Mrs Green mention the same man, in a Puritan's broad-brimmed black hat, nobody else in sight; Mrs Bennett has seen him too. For a while I can't walk across the bridge without thinking of the Puritan, and sometimes I steal glances from a distance as if I'd catch him off-guard, as if he'd only be crossing the bridge when he thinks I'm not looking, and even then I sense the sombre religious weight this figure brings in from the other side. Once or twice I go out before breakfast and step carefully to a point at the corner of the lawn where I can see straight through the gatehouse arch with bridge and church beyond it, my expectation of the man so strong it might have power to put him there. And there *is* somebody, approaching through the mist. I freeze in my tracks, every spring in me coiled tightly, and watch for the black glyph of the hat to appear, heart racing, until I realize that it's Mrs Upton herself arriving for work, in her soft wool hat, with her vinyl tartan shopping bag, shuffling in from the world.

o

In January 1781, encouraged by Walsh's work on electric fish, Luigi Galvani, Professor of Anatomy at the University of Bologna, began a series of experiments on frogs. In a laboratory equipped with friction machines and Leyden jars, Galvani dissected a frog so the thighs were entirely removed, leaving the animal's legs attached to the rest of its body by the sciatic nerves alone. 'Having in mind other things,' Galvani would report, 'I placed the frog on the same table as an electrical machine, so that the animal was completely separated from and removed from the machine's conductor. When one of my assistants by chance lightly applied the point of a scalpel to the inner crural nerves of the frog, suddenly all the muscles of the limbs were seen so to contract that they appeared to have fallen into violent tonic convulsions. Another assistant who was present when we were performing electrical experiments thought he observed that this phenomenon occurred when a spark was discharged from the conductor of the electrical machine.' Galvani asked his assistant to produce another spark from the device, and carefully applied his scalpel to the frog's exposed nerve. Once again, the frog's legs contracted.

Galvani went on experimenting with frogs and electricity. In April 1786, he took another of his prepared frogs onto the terrace of the Palazzo Zamboni in Bologna. He wanted to see if the animal would convulse in the same way when the source wasn't the artificial electricity of a machine, but the atmospheric electricity of clouds discharging in a storm. He placed the frog on a small table, a wire leading from its exposed nerves to the eaves as a makeshift conductor. 'Contractions,' Galvani would report, 'were obtained during lightning and even when lightning was not flashing.'

The following September, Galvani hung frogs from an iron railing by means of iron hooks that pierced their spinal cords. 'The hooks,' Galvani would write, 'touched the iron bar. And, lo and behold, the frogs began to display spontaneous, irregular and frequent movements.' Galvani recorded the same convulsions when the hooks were placed against other metals. However, 'other bodies which conducted electricity poorly or not at all, such as glass, gum, resin, stone, or wood did not give similar results; no such muscular contractions or movements could be seen.'

Galvani was convinced this third experiment proved that animals possessed their own electricity. The contractions were identical to electrical ones, yet there was no external electrical source – mechanical or atmospheric – to cause them. In his *Commentary on the Effects of Electricity on Muscular Motion*, published in 1791, Galvani proposed that animals possessed an intrinsic or 'indwelling' electricity. This 'Animal Electricity' emerged from the brain and was conducted to the muscles by the nerves. It was no longer necessary to think of nerves as tiny tubes that conveyed a mysterious fluid from the brain to the muscles to generate motion, and from the muscles to the brain to carry back sensations. These previously unidentified 'animal spirits' were in fact electricity.

Fifty years later the German physiologist Emil Du Bois-Reymond developed recording instruments (called galvanometers, in honour of Galvani) sensitive enough to detect electrical changes in nerves. In the two volumes of his *Investigations on Animal Electricity*, published in 1848 and 1849, Du Bois-Reymond showed that nerve impulses were invariably accompanied by electrical signals. His experiments were repeated by Richard Caton, lecturer in physiology at the Royal Infirmary School of Medicine in Liverpool. Inspired by Du Bois-Reymond's proof of the electrical nature of nerve impulses, Caton wondered if there might also be electrical signals in the brain. In the early 1870s, using electrodes fixed to the skulls of rabbits, cats and monkeys, Caton attempted to record electrical activity in the brain. 'In every brain hitherto examined,' he would write in his preliminary report, 'the galvanometer has indicated the existence of electric currents.'

o

When Mum proposed an outing – an expedition to Oxford, or Leamington Spa, or Warwick Castle – the ladies exchanged glances in the kitchen, reluctant to be first to commit to the scheme. The minutes before departure were charged with heightened expectation, everyone dressed up, Mrs Upton and Mrs Green wearing brooches in their wool coats, one hand on their hats as they climbed into the two-tone Volkswagen camper van, white on top, cream yellow below. The Dormobile had a sliding passenger door, two gas rings, a tiny sink under a veneer lid and a roof you could unlock and extend upwards for standing room: with the roof up, the Dormobile looked like a van wearing a chef's hat. You could slot wood panels in and rearrange faded red cushions to make a double bed, and on holiday I'd sleep in a bunk in the extended roof, condensation running down the striped waterproof canvas that connected the roof to the van body, my parents below, Dad snoring, the wool filling of my sleeping bag gathering in heavy clumps like clots in its circulation.

Joyce sat up front next to my mother and I sat in the back with Mrs Upton, Mrs Green and Mrs Dancer, shopping bags on their laps.

'Are we all set?' my mother asked.

'Why? Aren't we there yet?' Mrs Dancer replied, spirits lifting as the van slipped through the gatehouse arch, crossing the bridge into the wider world.

Mrs Upton mentioned May Day celebrations. Mrs Green picked this up straightaway: remembering how they'd put flowers in their hair, she raised her hand to her head in a quick mime of herself as a girl, checking the blooms above her ears.

'You had your clothes baskets, didn't you, Joyce, with all your dolls in the middle?'

'That's right,' Joyce said, turning to look at the ladies in the back.

'And then you'd sing,' Mrs Upton said. 'What was it? Something about, "Do you like my garland?" I can't remember it all. Something about "my garland".'

' "This is the first of May," ' Mrs Green began. ' "Do you like my garland?" '

'We used to put thin dresses on, and you know what the first of May's like – we used to be shivering. But we'd be singing, the lot of us.'

The group dispersed in the department store. I passed Joyce on the escalators, standing still on the moving stairs; I was going up and she was going down; she didn't notice me – she seemed dazed by the bright array of clothes, shoes, furnishings, kitchenware, people hurrying in all directions.

Mrs Upton and Mrs Green were wearing soft wool hats; Mrs Dancer smoked roll-ups; Mrs Upton held forth on the way home. She'd use a proverb and then elaborate on it, in case you didn't understand: 'A rolling stone gathers no moss. If a stone's moving, the moss won't be able to grow on it. No moss at all: it can't get started, you see.'

My mother had bought some earrings.

'Very nice,' Mrs Upton said. 'Well, you've got to make the best of yourself, now you're getting on.'

They compared purchases.

'Did you get yourself something nice, Joyce?'

'I did, thank you, Mrs Green. I got a nice drop of soap.'

o

Sometimes, after I'd gone to bed, I'd hear my mother's viola scales drifting up the stairs, each scale like someone coming up the stairs then going down them again on second thoughts. She stole ten minutes here or there to practise, playing the same pieces over and over, almost always Bach, the Cello Suites and Brandenburg Concertos in transcriptions by Watson Forbes, stepping into them as if they were familiar rooms, dependable and comforting, the white Anglepoise craning over her shoulder like someone trying to read the time signatures.

What I liked best was the sound of her tuning the viola, the way she'd loosen the peg a fraction before bringing it up to the correct pitch, as if it was only by being first slightly mistaken in something that you could see the right answer clearly. Sometimes I got impatient and tried to distract her by talking or playing rowdy sabotage notes on the piano, even waving my hand between her and the music to get her attention, to make her stop, because I thought it was time for supper or I was simply bored of mooching about on my own, but she resisted: she didn't want to leave the music; she wanted longer in that private room, away from everything, playing each piece as if she were trying to say how much she loved it.

At first, it wasn't music itself but the paraphernalia gathered round music that drew me in: the velvet-covered clip-on pad that cushioned the collarbone; the loose horse-hair strands you had to pluck from the bow's tip and heel; the grooved resin cube you drew along the bow, fine dust lifting in the lampglare. Left to my own devices, I often ended up in the music room. If I stood on the chair I could open the lid of the Broadwood upright and peer in at strings drawn vertically like a harp's, a rank of felt hammers posed against them, cobweb strands swagged from bolt to bolt. My mother's viola lay in the plush of its case with the lid open, like someone on display in a funeral home. I could touch the scrolled neck, black tuning pegs and f-holes, the delicate maple bridge with notches the strings bit into; I could smell the eccentric mixture of linseed oil and Acqua di Selva eau-de-cologne Mum's teacher had encouraged her to rub into the wood.

In a compartment in the case she kept a tuning fork, a piece of ingenious cutlery that hummed a perfect note when you struck it on the oak chest and held it close to your ear. Touch the butt to a hard, flat surface and the prongs would sing the same insistent A out loud, as if they'd discovered a note that was already in the room and were merely revealing it to you by pulling off a dustsheet. Best of all was the small Wittner metronome Mum used to furnish a tempo – a cream-coloured plastic hutch with a wand like a clock hand on the front, a round fixed weight at the foot of the wand,

and a second weight you could slide up and down to adjust the speed, strange words – *Allegro*, *Andante*, *Adagio* – printed alongside.

The metronome fascinated me; I couldn't keep my hands off it. Mum told me it wasn't a toy and left it out of reach on top of the piano, but it wasn't hard to clamber from chair to keyboard and bring myself eye-level with it. I turned the key at the side to wind the clockwork, unhitched the wand from the plastic clasp and set it rocking from side to side like a hypnotist's finger, a loud tock marking each extremity. If you pushed the sliding weight down to the bottom, the metronome went berserk, wagging as fast as it could; if you slid the weight to the tip of the scale, the wand swung through lugubrious arcs, sombre grandfather-clock beats echoing in the stone vaults. Suddenly it seemed the time you set by the metronome was *actual* time, and that your life passed more slowly or quickly as you slid the weight up and down the scale, the music room a world that turned at whatever speed you judged appropriate. The tuning fork and metronome granted supernatural powers. The day's pitch and time-keeping were in my hands.

o

I never asked why our house was open to the public or saw anything unusual in the fact that thousands of strangers walked past our bedrooms and peered in through the kitchen window each year. I understood there had to be money to pay Mr and Mrs Dancer, Mrs Upton, Mrs Green, Harry

Bennett and the guides, that all the expenses of upkeep and repair had to be met somehow. But my parents didn't see it as mere necessity. The house didn't just belong to us: it was part of the country's heritage, the world's, and our task was to care for it for as long as we were here, and do our best to leave it in good health for future generations. 'We're stewards,' Dad told visitors. He and my mother wanted to look after the house on behalf of everyone who might one day appreciate it, in a month's time or a hundred years.

It was ours, and more than ours. I watched the bone structures of marquees going up on the lawns for receptions and church fetes, guy ropes pegged taut, Mrs Parsley, Mr and Mrs Howarth, Mr and Mrs Woodhouse, Mrs Hopkins, Mrs Knight and Mr and Mrs Lewis carrying boxes and folding tables, setting up book stalls, cake stalls, jumble sales and lucky dips. You could try the raffle, tombola, hoopla and skittles or guess how many pennies were in the jar while two freckled sisters in sashed white blouses and tartan skirts danced nimbly over swords and a band played on the lawn, woodwind and brass and drums, the musicians smiling at each other as if the tempo were a seam of happiness they'd all just chanced upon. I roamed the stalls with proprietorial licence, giddy with novelty and festival, but at the same time resentful of this intrusion, the way everything most familiar to me had been transformed by show and bustle. But Rich was in his element, hurling balls at the coconut shy with such exaggerated force they thwacked into the yellow tarpaulin leaving dimples still visible in late afternoon, exchanging greetings with guides, church wardens and farmers, his hand on Mrs Dancer's shoulder to secure her attention while he told a joke, their faces alight with laughter.

Now there's a fiddle and accordion playing somewhere, the stave clacks and shin-ringing of Morris men – eight of them following the band onto the grass, in white trousers and shirts, straw hats and buckled black shoes. A jester with rouged cheeks brandished a stick, an inflated pig's bladder attached to the end. He was hitting people over the head with it, children especially, and I ran round the back of the marquee to get away, but then a huge bear reared up on its hind legs and roared and stepped towards me. I raised my hand to my mouth in fright as the bear, much taller than a man, towered over me: I could see its yellow teeth and hard, grey-brown claws. It wore the same white shirt and three-quarter-length white trousers as the Morris dancers and I didn't know what it was doing out here, roaming freely; I didn't see the man's eyes glinting at the back of the bear's mouth, where the tonsils should have been; it didn't occur to me that this was a man in the skin of a bear; I just recognized something wild and fierce, a monster the out-side world had smuggled in among tents and caravans. I ran, yelling, and didn't look back over my shoulder until I found Mum waiting outside the Great Hall, the next group gathering for a tour.

I tagged along on tours and so began to absorb the facts and stories of each room. King James I and King Edward VII had slept in the Kings' Chamber; the hand-painted

Chinese wallpaper came with extra butterflies to paste over the lines between strips; the Council Chamber was called 'the room with no ears' because it had three outside walls and a trusted guard stationed at the door. Mum pinned a GUIDE badge to my T-shirt and I stood in the Dining Room or Long Gallery with an eye out for burglars, hoping no one would approach me with questions I'd have no way of answering: Who painted that picture above the fireplace? How old were the cups and saucers on the chest of drawers? Sometimes I knew the answer because I'd heard my parents repeat it so often: the round table was Burmese rosewood, the glossy black seats on the chairs were made of horsehair, the black leather buckets would have been filled with sand and used in the eighteenth century as fire-extinguishers. There were braided ropes across doorways and staircases but I ducked under them with casual immunity, ignoring the *Private: No Entry* signs to pass from this public realm back into our quiet private spaces, Rich sitting upstairs in front of *Sunday Grandstand*, Joel Garner bowling in a John Player League game, bells ringing trackside as huddles of long-distance runners leaned into final laps.

Every now and then my mother managed to persuade Rich to wear a GUIDE badge too and go on duty just for twenty minutes while one of the regular guides took a tea break, and he seemed to swell into himself as he accepted the task, exalted by responsibility. The badge singled him out as a figure of authority, a source of privileged insight, and if someone came to him with a question he'd listen with solemn concentration, his forehead all ridges and furrows; he'd take it in, say 'Just wait here one second,' then stride purposefully down the Long Gallery, pounding the floorboards, engaging our mother's attention by resting his hand on her shoulder, even if she's in the middle of another conversation, and saying, 'Mum. *Mum.*'

'Wait a minute, darling,' she says.

'But it's *very important*,' Rich replies.

'But I'm just talking to these people, you see.'

'But you don't understand. I just have to ask you something. It's *very* important.'

He presses down on her shoulder for emphasis.

o

Perhaps there was no need to go out into the world when such a pageant was passing through – gardeners, photographers, anglers, actors, craftsmen, historians, builders, the house a town through which circus caravans were endlessly travelling. English Civil War enthusiasts arrived in visored Roundhead helmets, breastplates and backplates over tan leather undercoats, floppy black boots with authentic-looking buckles on the arches. They pitched cannons on the lawn and packed wadding, powder and shot down musket barrels while others crouched in porcupine formations, pikes rayed outwards, gunpowder smoke drifting over the moat, the dirty polystyrene plugs they'd used for cannon-balls floating against the banks for days afterwards. Sealed Knot re-enactment hobbyists dressed Dad as a Cromwellian leader and I watched these armoured strangers shackle his wrists and ankles in actual manacles and lead him off our encircled island to imprisonment and torture, chains dragging on the gravel, a situation made even more confusing by the fact that one of his captors presented the children's TV show I watched on Saturday mornings: I didn't understand what he was doing taking my father away.

I learned about longbows and haunted the arrow-slit windows in the gatehouse and along the battlements, scoping the field, sighting along my outstretched arm, drawing the string back to my ear. I learned about Prince Rupert's army attacking the house after the Battle of Edge Hill in 1642 and sometimes I heard cannon booms and hoof-thunder coming from the park. Actual cannonballs sat on a table in the Council Chamber like messages from gravity: they'd been salvaged from the moat and even with two hands I couldn't lift them. I walked across the bridge to find fleets of classic Austins, Fords or Jaguars arrayed in summer rallies by the water – starting handles, exterior klaxons, badges on radiator grilles, a sleek, buffed gleam-show materializing where the park flattened close to the moat, oaks leaning over the cars, Rich introducing himself to rally organizers – 'It's *so* nice to see you!' – entirely content, caught up in gala feeling, red and white bunting looped round the Tannoy. When the dark fury-moods took over, my mother and father pitched themselves between him and the visitors; they made themselves tyres slung round boats to buffer hulls against the wharf; they had to protect both the outsiders and Rich himself from the damage he was capable of inflicting, steering him away from the scene, distracting him like a child. Sometimes they were worried not that he'd lash out at anyone but that he'd tire them with excessive solicitude, the loving weight of his hand on your shoulder, Leeds monologue blurring to a drone.

o

In the late 1860s the psychiatrist Gustav Fritsch and the anatomist Eduard Hitzig began applying electricity directly to the brain. Working at a dressing table in Hitzig's house in Berlin, the two physicians removed sections of the skulls of dogs under ether anaesthesia, exposing one hemisphere of the cerebral cortex. Using platinum electrodes with pinpoint terminals (to reduce the chance of damaging tissue or its blood supply), they gave the dogs' brains small electric shocks, measuring the stimulus intensity by first touching the electrodes onto their own tongues. Applying the electrodes to different regions of the cortex, Fritsch and Hitzig found that stimulating one specific area near the front of the brain led to an immediate movement of the forepaw on the opposite side of the dog's body. They soon identified a corresponding hind-paw region, as well as face and neck areas. They had found the place, they wrote, 'where the spirit enters the body'.

In *On the Electrical Excitability of the Cerebrum*, published in 1870, Fritsch and Hitzig described a specialized motor cortex: a particular region of the brain responsible for body movement. 'A part of the convexity of the hemisphere of the brain of the dog is motor,' they declared. 'Another part is not motor. The motor part, in general, is more in front, the non-motor part more behind. By electrical stimulation of the motor part, one obtains combined muscular contractions of the opposite side of the body.' Increasing the strength of the current, they added, led to 'generalized movements on both sides of the body'; in two cases these movements 'developed into generalized epileptic attacks.'

In 1875, David Ferrier acknowledged 'the discovery of the electric excitability of the brain by Fritsch and Hitzig.' In his laboratory at the West Riding Lunatic Asylum, in Yorkshire, Ferrier had exposed and stimulated the brains of anaesthetized rabbits, cats, dogs, jackals, pigeons, rats and monkeys. He too found that electrical stimulation of one hemisphere of an animal's brain caused violent convulsions of muscle groups on the opposite side of its body; that the hand, leg and facial movements of epileptic seizures could be mimicked by stimulating certain areas of the cortex; and that bigger seizures could be induced by increasing the strength of the current. Fritsch and Hitzig had described five cortical 'centres' for various movements in dogs; Ferrier identified fifteen motor centres in monkeys: fifteen areas of the brain where movement could be triggered by electrical stimulation.

In January 1874, while Ferrier carried out his animal experiments in Yorkshire, the American physician Roberts Bartholow began treating a thirty-year-old woman named Mary Rafferty at his clinic in Cincinnati, Ohio. Cancer had eroded part of her skull, exposing an area of her brain to open air.

Nothing could be done to save her. Bartholow approached his patient with a proposed experiment. He wanted to stimulate the exposed part of her brain with an electric current, as Fritsch, Hitzig and Ferrier had done with their animal subjects. Rafferty agreed. Bartholow inserted two needle electrodes into the exposed left side. 'When the circuit was closed,' he would report, 'distinct muscular con-tractions occurred in the right arm and leg. The arm was thrown out, the fingers extended, and the leg was projected forward. The muscles of the neck were thrown into action, and the head was strongly deflected to the right.'

Bartholow inserted the electrodes a second time into Mary Rafferty's brain. He closed the circuit and increased the current. 'When communication was made with the needles,' the doctor reported, 'her countenance exhibited great distress, and she began to cry. Very soon the left hand was extended as if in the act of taking hold of some object in front of her; the arm presently was agitated with clonic spasm; her eyes became fixed, with pupils widely dilated; lips were blue, and she frothed at the mouth; her breathing became stertorous; she lost consciousness, and was violently convulsed on the left side . . . She returned to consciousness in twenty minutes from the beginning of the attack, and complained of some weakness and vertigo.'

Bartholow had induced a seizure in a human being.

o

Early in December, Dad took me and Richard to find a Christmas tree. Rich had to be coaxed away from the television: he got up with a sigh as if he was doing us a special favour. I was bundled in wool hat, scarf and gloves, two pairs of thick socks on under my gumboots; Rich wore his Leeds bobble hat, his thin leather jacket zipped up. We fetched saws from Bert's shed in the stables – a new orange-handled bow saw and an older plain saw with a wide, rusting blade that flexed with a metallic squelch when you waved it – and strode up the park toward Stafford Wood, the ground hard underfoot. Soon I was lagging behind, Dad in his tweed cap setting the pace, Rich beside him, the bow saw under his arm like a lyre, their breath visible in small discrete clouds over their heads like speech balloons in comic strips. I ran to catch them up.

Dad stopped to inspect trees he'd planted, each in a neat square pen of post-and-rail and wire fencing to keep sheep and cattle off, wire mesh or plastic spiral guards round the trunks to protect against rabbits. He laid his forearms along the top rail and leaned against it, admiring the young tree, a few curling dry leaves still attached, then the three of us turned to look down at the house and gatehouse and crenellated curtain wall, outlines honed to rimy sharpness in the cold. The moat had started to freeze: ducks congregated in open patches; a heron rose from the frost-white bank below us and flew over the Sor Brook and Lower Quarters.

'There he goes!' Rich said, his surly TV mood forgotten.

Once in the wood we started looking for a Norway spruce among beech, cherry, holly, elder and hawthorn.

'I think this is the one,' Dad said. 'Don't you, Rich?'

Richard considered it solemnly, frowning beneath the Leeds hat, looking round to rule out other spruces before offering his agreement.

'I think so, yes.'

He pulled off the sheepskin gloves and placed them carefully on a heap of bramble, side by side, pressing them down to make sure they didn't slide off while Dad shouldered in among spruce branches and made the first cut, just half an inch to get things started. He straightened and handed the saw to Richard.

Dad always let Rich fell the tree. Even as Rich took the bow saw in his right hand he grew and strengthened with responsibility. He bent and got in close to the trunk, fitted the blade to the notch and punched the saw forward.

'That's it, Rich,' Dad said. 'Let the saw do the work.'

But Rich didn't hear him. He seemed to be pitting his own strength against the tree's: when the saw got stuck he didn't reverse the stroke gently and start again, he applied brute force and wrangled it from the groove. I touched the blade and drew my hand back quickly from the heat.

Rich took off his Leeds hat and placed it on the bramble heap, then removed his leather jacket and looked round for somewhere to hang it. He wouldn't just throw it down any old how: he found a beech branch that forked at the end and fitted the leather jacket over it, one prong of the fork in each shoulder, all this carried out with slow-motion fastidiousness while Dad and I looked on.

'Right,' he said, taking up the saw again.

Whenever he was fully engaged in some physical task, his tongue dropped in front of his bottom teeth and pushed out his cheek below the corner of his mouth like a wad of dentist's cotton wool. Certain epilepsy drugs can cause unusual facial movements called extra-pyramidal movements, and for a while Richard's pills caused him to circle his jaw unconsciously, as if he were chewing a cud, his lower lip enlarged and blubbery, hanging forward. Now, his tongue already probing his cheek in concentration, he leaned into the branches, fitted the blade and wrestled the saw back and forth until there was only an inch of trunk intact. We heard the first splinter-cracks as the tree teetered.

'All right, Rich,' Dad said. 'Stand back!'

Richard watched with a lumberjack's brawny pride as the spruce fell in a rush of needles. I had the junior task of stripping brash from the trunk with a folding pruning saw.

Dad and Rich heaved the spruce onto their shoulders and walked it down the park back to the house. So this was our Christmas tree in the Great Hall under suits of Spanish armour, an arsenal of pikes, rapiers, muskets and broadswords round the walls, pinnacles dangling from the plaster ceiling. Mum used a halberd to hang lights over the tinfoil apex star. I ran back and forth along the Groined Passage between the huge cold hangar-space of the Great Hall and the warm kitchen. The broad stone stairs up from the passage to the Chapel were almost seven hundred years old and each step had its own distinct undulation, the stone worn in patterns of smooth dip and hollow as if water had been flowing down it, no two steps the same, the arched chapel door left open so that from the bottom of the stairs you'd look up through dark to a high, bright window. Those undulations were so pronounced you felt your body tilted one way and then the other as you walked up or down; there were stone handrails on both sides of the stairs, buffed and shiny and cold, and it was a Christmas game for some-one to stand at the top and send wrapped sweets hurtling down the stone chute while you waited at the bottom and tried to catch them. The spiral staircase that's sunk through the medieval house like a mineshaft had a stone handrail too, burnished to marble gloss by hands running up and down it, and at Christmas the handrail became a helter-skelter, curved and frictionless like a bobsleigh run, sweets gathering speed as they corkscrewed down.

Black iron breastplates hung along the Groined Passage, lamps held out on wrought-iron stanchions shaped like dragons, vaults meeting in pointed arches overhead, faces and symbols carved into corbels at the base of each one: a woman in a wimple and buttoned bodice; a horned ram with a long fleece; vine leaves round a bunch of grapes; a rabbit eating peas; a pig in oak leaves; a salamander with a knotted tail; a muzzled dog; a monster with wings, talons and a unicorn's horn. If you were climbing the west stairs and paused at just the right moment, high up, you could look out at the next bay jutting into the Ladies' Garden and see another face, a stonemason's joke, a human face adrift in stone, invisible to any casual eye. In the Groined Passage I was more interested in the breastplates, the curve sharpening to a ridge at the front as if to cleave a way through battle: on some you could see the dimple-impacts of musket balls. But sometimes I looked up and a corbel caught me by surprise, an unexpected grace or ferocity that restored the other stone faces to prominence and strangeness: I felt their gaze on my skin like a pressure of light, and ran for the door.

Christmas afternoon, light starting to fade, Dad poured brandy into a jam jar and screwed the lid shut. We put on coats, hats and gumboots, ready for a walk. Rich was watching the James Bond and didn't want to go outside, but just as we were disappearing into the gatehouse arch I heard his size-eleven gumboots thumping the turf and turned to see him sprinting to catch up. We followed the Sor Brook east below the village, cricket-bat willows along the banks, a veteran staghead oak in the field below the Woad Mill, the lights of the dairy buildings ahead of us like decorations in the willow branches. The big green door slid back on rollers, and then it was one step up onto a concrete floor wet from hosing, into a dream of pipes and valves, glass collection jars, pump vibration and hum, a huge milk tank in the centre of the room, a shining steel door on top that rang like a cymbal when you raised it. The tank had an ice jacket to chill the contents; my father or mother lifted me so I could peer into that room of milk, stirred by paddles; when I got my head right in it was like looking down on a lake of milk in a steel cave; I wondered what it would be like to slide in and swim figures-of-eight round the paddles.

Ken had the Christmas shift in the milking parlour. He was in the concrete trench between two ranks of stalls, wearing a boiler suit and rubber boots. Vapour rose off the cows, the floor awash with cow urine, milk, hosewater and iodine; you could hear cows exhaling like bellows through the whirr and throb of machinery, heads thudding in feed bins, dairy nuts rattling from the loft down metal chutes, the clangour of stall gates, a faint jangle from Ken's radio in the heart of the din. My father said something but I couldn't hear him beyond the pump and cow rumpus, the steel clang and judder. Dad reached into his pocket and produced the jam jar of brandy, holding it out towards Ken as if he were handing a sample to his doctor. Ken unscrewed the lid, sniffed and took a sip, then screwed the lid back on and shouted that he'd save it for later. I turned to look back over the dairy's elaborate plumbing. Some of the pipes were clear glass and you could actually see the milk bubbling and sloshing through; unused milking clusters dangled like octopuses from the rails; the iodine and water hoses had pistol attachments at the ends and I imagined portable versions I could draw from holsters. A cow raised its head from a feed

bin and mooed loudly; Rich turned to it and yelled, laughing, 'Shut your mouth!' He was in high spirits again: when
we left the dairy the light had almost gone, but Rich spied
a loose stone on the concrete forecourt, kicked it with a full
swing of his black gumboot and celebrated this last-minute
winner for Leeds by punching his right fist into the sky.

o

I didn't question the world as I found it: our wide moat and
gatehouse tower, the medieval chapel above the kitchen,
the huge uninhabited rooms to the west and the parade of
strangers that passed through them each year; the way our
house was divided into two parts, one private, the other
open to public view. I didn't question my brother's seizures
or the frightening and unpredictable swings of his mood
from gentleness and warmth to opposition and violence –
these too were just facts I grew up among, how things were.

Our Igloo tent had an architecture of brown inflatable
tubes with blue canvas sections between them, and along
with a dedicated pump it gathered dust all winter in the
stables loft among chair stacks, bicycles, floodlights, tobog-
gans and wire crayfish traps. There was a peculiar room up
here with nothing in it but glass-fronted cabinets of stuffed
birds no one had a use or home for: one devoted to waders,
one to egrets, one to kingfishers and hummingbirds, one
to pheasants, grouse and snipe. A peacock had a cabinet to
itself, tail-fan spread in display. The birds had enamel beads
for eyes and stood in rigid grass, draped with cobwebs;

they seemed alive and dead at the same time; I had to force myself to open the door and step into that airless mausoleum gloom. I went in one morning and found a jackdaw, a living bird, flying round and round over the cabinets of dead ones. I watched from the doorway, thinking a stuffed bird had come back to life before I realized the jackdaw had got in by the chimney. The cabinet devoted to five white egrets had lost its glass pane, and the jackdaw landed among them, in the fake scenery, its head twitching while the dead white birds stared at it.

You needed two to lug that Igloo tent down the hollow wood steps with white plastic treads on the front edges, across the gravel onto the lawn that rose slightly at the stables end – a swell you wouldn't notice if you hadn't spent years doing forward rolls or chasing balls across it. Rich and Martin carried the tent out and dropped it on the grass while my mother and I looked on. We pegged it out foursquare and then Martin fitted the foot pump and began to inflate the tent, the Igloo's brown structural tubes first thickening then lifting from the blue. Slowly the brown spars rose to their apex, blue canvas stretched between the arches, and as Martin kept working the foot pump the tubes hardened and locked into place, the tent domed like an actual igloo, the unzipped door hanging open. This August afternoon was sultry and close, the air thicker than usual, planes trawling through it like swimmers, and we were all so engaged in pitching the tent – absorbed in the way it seemed to materialize of its own accord, lifting from the

square of crumpled material as if it were waking up to the
possibility of being a dome – that none of us noticed
the storm approaching.

I'd felt the whole house shaken by thunder at night:
windows rattling in loose frames, wind buffeting through
attic rooms, a creaking like an old ship's hull timbers, as if
the house were a medium for the wind to hear its own voice
in, a register in which details of the Beaufort Scale were
caught and sounded. The church spire beyond the moat was
hospitable to lightning: the line of a conductor snaked
down from the tip; one strike left a black hole beneath the
cockerel weathervane as if a cannonball had crashed in;
steeplejacks rappelling up the pinnacle got a view of moat
and castle none of us intimates were privy to. The gatehouse
was another temptation. One night lightning picked a
single battlement and knocked it clean out, and we woke to
a gap as if someone we'd known for ages had lost a front
tooth in a brawl. But I'd never been stranded outside in one
of these disturbances.

It's exciting to be standing out there on the lawn as this
storm approaches. There's no rain yet but the light has a
pewter tint, trees and buildings rimmed with metal. When
the rain comes, we duck into the Igloo and Martin zips
the door shut. Soon the rain's pounding the canvas dome
and it feels as if we're huddled inside that hard tattoo thrum,
a shell of noise. The first thunder is a far-off tympanum
roll; lightning brightens the tent canvas as if someone's
taking pictures of it. Mum has us counting seconds between

lightning strikes and thunder rolls; she tells us this is how you measure a storm's distance, each second a mile. We all join in, shouting *ONE one-thousand TWO one-thousand THREE one-thousand* like parachutists gauging when to pull the ripcord, and so track the storm's progress over Hook Norton, Shenington, Epwell and Shutford, until it's right overhead and there's no delay to count, just a quick brightening of canvas as thunder cracks and echoes. The counting was my mother's distraction technique and without it I'm frightened, but Martin says the rubber in the Igloo's support tubes is proof against lightning, and then he unzips the flap again for a face-to-face with the storm. Cool air rushes in, and between my two brothers I glimpse grey metal light blurred with rain and the house with its 'I am!' of chimneys suddenly lit by a many-forked jaggedness that lingers on some rear panel of my eyes for seconds afterwards. Rich gazes out exhilarated, his face shining, nothing between him and the storm.

TWO

I WENT TO BOARDING SCHOOL when I was eight. I didn't mind: I liked the gregarious, crowded days. At home, I didn't have neighbours I could call on, or friends further down the street. I spent hours walking the moat banks, spotting herons, watching for pike in the shallows. I read books and comics. I waited in the kitchen while Mrs Upton, Mrs Green and Mr and Mrs Dancer had their hot drinks, Joyce on her high stool like a lifeguard. I sat in the hidden chestnut throne, climbed the holly ladder to Harry Bennett's tree house, and rode my bike across the bridge and cattle grid, accelerating through the park, taking the single-track road to the farms at Fulling Mill and Broughton Grounds.

I had a castle to explore whenever I wanted. But I was still afraid of the other end. I had to dare myself to leave our familiar quarters and walk alone through those cold historical spaces beyond the music room. The latch click echoed in the vaults when I opened the door into the Groined Passage. I'd take a deep breath and dash for the Great Hall, bursting into its expanse and brightness. I'd jump the red Shutford Plush sofas and climb onto deep window ledges behind leather fire buckets; I'd squeeze the triggers on muskets and try the weight of breastplates and Roundhead helmets; I'd brandish basket-hilt swords and advance on suits of Spanish armour in the west wall niches.

But I hadn't ventured into the other end just to linger in the Great Hall. I had a goal, a destination. I ran up the east stairs past the portrait of Admiral Swanton to a landing off the Long Gallery, and stopped at the foot of a narrow, winding staircase in a dark corner by the laundry cupboards. The stairs led to the Barracks. I didn't go up them straight-away. I played for time, opening the cupboard's heavy oak doors, peering in on shelves lined with wallpaper offcuts, filled with bedraggled eiderdowns, linen and blanket stacks, plastic bags stuffed with chintz scraps and upholstery tassels and braid. I'd seen Mum fold old pillows in half and pitch them like basketballs into the top shelf; I'd climbed from one shelf to the next as if they were ledges on a sheer, difficult section of the mountain. But my thoughts kept turning to the Barracks. I was almost there. I closed the cupboard doors and faced the corner.

The spiral stairs were triangles of rough, grooved elm that boomed under my feet like bass drums. They led right up into the roof, into attic spaces known as the Barracks since the seventeenth century, because soldiers had slept here during the Civil War, and anyway the word 'attic' was hardly adequate for this mysterious gable province of locked rooms off a corridor hung with paintings of ill-proportioned racehorses and guardsmen in bearskin hats, square-rigged ships listing through sea battles.

The air smelled of stone, wood, dust, damp cotton and paper; deathwatch beetles riddled the beams; grey light seeped through skylights almost opaque with cobwebs and guano. I imagined I'd got into the hold of an inverted ship – a cargo of tea chests, leather trunks and suitcases embossed with initials, blazoned with ocean-going labels (Cunard Line, White Star Line) and stacked among defunct lamps with crumpled shades, antique Attenhofer skis, dressmakers' wicker dummies and golf clubs in slender white bags, rust on the heads of Spalding cushion-neck irons. I opened drawers and doors and lifted dust-sheets, finding junk-sale arrays of bowls, jugs, candlesticks and andirons, and rigid leather gauntlets, riding boots hardened round wooden boot trees, a shin-high herd of carved elephants, mixed stooks of walking sticks and sabres, and stationery boxes, Victorian wage books and photograph albums, and bundles of post-cards and letters strewn with bat droppings.

Some objects drew me back, again and again. A cherry-wood cabinet had four slim drawers divided into square compartments, each home to two or three birds' eggs in nests of white tissue paper and cotton wool. Pale blue, brown, speckled grey, with pinholes where Victorian collec-tors had blown them, some of the eggs were part-crushed, collapsed in on themselves, but among each batch lay a strip of white card, nibbled by mites so it had the per-forated edges of postage stamps, the names of birds in a fine, miniature hand. I checked the drawers of eggs and then looked for the drum, the kind a cadet wears strapped to his chest in a marching band, its skin gashed on one side, a flap hanging off; when I bashed the taut skin with my fist a dull thud, just beneath tone, rolled down the Barracks corridor like a tyre. In a black metal case among chairs draped in dustsheets I found a naval hat, the real thing, black felt trimmed with gold braid, a downy white plume arching off the crest. I put it on and drew a sabre to lunge and parry down the passageway, cutlass sound-effects in the gloom.

I stopped in front of the secret door. It was invisible, flush to the partition wall, no giveaway handle or outline in the half-dark: I had to find it with my fingers. This disguise, and the fact that it was always shut, gave the door and what lay behind it a threshold power. I thought the door was closed not to keep people out but to keep something in, and usually I ran past it if I'd gone up to the Barracks on my own to try the lids on chests or rummage through suitcases for letters from the war. I was afraid of it. The Barracks itself was frightening enough, so much of the *old* hoarded in the dark, the kitchen's life-bustle so far away, out of earshot. In the Barracks I heard myself breathe and imagined objects coming to life as soon as my concentration faltered, as if I'd passed into some other jurisdiction where the influence of familiar household gods no longer applied. The secret door gave access to a still stranger dimension. I'd never opened it or gone beyond it on my own. Now I stood in front of it, breathing quickly.

'Hello?' I said.

I put my ear to the door. I could hear something moving on the other side.

'Hello?' I said.

o

Richard's moustache was a fixture by now. He took pride in it.

'You're looking very dashing, Richard,' Mrs Dancer told him. 'With your moustache.'

'Well, I don't know about that!'

I recognized the happy tension in his face, as if he were unsure whether to suppress or unleash his smile.

His hair was black, wavy and dense, no flyaway strands, his eyebrows thick as moustaches over brown-green eyes. His beard grew quickly; the wiry black thickets in his nostrils needed regular trimming.

He'd started to smoke a pipe but hadn't mastered the technique. When we watched TV together, the room soon filled with smoke: I peered through drifts to make out the picture. Rich always sat close to the TV, on a fine-legged chair that looked delicate beneath him, leaning forward so the back legs lifted from their footprints in the yellow carpet, setting his elbows on his knees and resting his chin on a plinth of laced fingers. Concentrating, he began to rock back and forth, chair joints creaking, factory billows of smoke escaping his nose and mouth, thickening the local atmosphere. He sat up straight and banged the pipe like a judge's gavel on the brown earthenware bowl he used as an ashtray. He held pouches of pungent flavoured tobaccos open beneath my nose and urged me to sniff, getting my nose in the pouch, tobacco strands like whiskers against my skin.

'Go on! Smell that!' he urged, smiling, impatient for my reaction to the coffee, rum and raisin or whisky and caramel blends.

Sometimes I'd come across him in the garden, wearing a wool cardigan and slippers, standing on the grass, keeping an eye out for herons or watching the rooks, pipe cupped in his right hand or clamped between his teeth, and he'd look like a retired schoolteacher from the 1950s, trousers belted high on his tummy. But then there was his face, his straight nose with the moustache beneath it, his strong, noble brow and cheekbones and jaw — a face from an ancient coin, handsome even when drugs caused his lower lip to fatten and hang off his mouth, or an epic fourteen-hour sleep left him puffy, his eyes bleared with dreaming.

He arranged white pipe cleaners and scraping tools on his bedside table; he insisted we stop at the tobacconist's on the way to the station so he could stock up on tobacco and lighter fuel. A long curtain wall topped with battlements ran out at an angle from the gatehouse and you could tell if Rich was walking on the far side by the steam-train clouds of smoke his pipe produced. Inside, he banged the pipe on the earthenware bowl, abrupt auctioneer raps to clear the last flecks of ash, to get the thing clean. Soon the pipe's repertoire of new sounds (the *rap rap rap* of the chamber on the earthenware dish, the lid-flip and rasp of the angle-flame Zippo, the scratch of the cleaning tool, the blasts he blew through the stem to clear the airway, cheeks puffing like a trumpeter's) included a distinctive cough, a chesty two-part motif, a rising *harrrupp* followed by a descending *harrroomm*, a smoker's cough that made me worry for the state of his lungs. But nobody considered taking his pipe away: more than pleasure, it was a form of autonomy, free from institutional interference, with its own private codes and rituals, its own dexterities to master and demonstrate.

He liked to smoke in the drawing room. In the evening Mum sat at one end of the sofa, next to her sewing table. Rich had made a cotton-reel holder in a woodwork class, six thin dowels in a disc of pine, sanded smooth, reels stacked four or five to a dowel with loose threads dangling off and needles secured in the bind. The holder had pride of place on the sewing table, next to a cream-shaded china lamp, a drawer underneath filled with buttons, name-tapes, thimbles, pop fasteners, hooks and eyes, needle kits in see-through plastic sachets and a sharp-pointed tool for unpicking stitches. Dad sat opposite, re-reading favourite books in his mother's small Everyman editions – Trollope, Tolstoy, Stendhal, George Eliot and Henry James – in the light from a second lamp on the chest of drawers, the mantel clock ticking, the sound of small metal trinkets shifting in compartments as Mum opened the drawer beside her, the fire rustling and cracking like someone walking in a wood.

Rich was drawn to the fire. He claimed the prerogative of kneeling where the yellow carpet met the stone forecourt of the grate to nestle a paraffin lighter cube in ash and build the logs around it. He disappeared into the small, ordered world of the task, working with slow-motion thoroughness, not just leaning one log against another but pressing it firmly into place, jamming it in, as if to be sure it would stick, as if the logs were conspiring among themselves to subvert the project and needed to be secured, nothing left to chance. Then he fished the Zippo from his pocket and rolled his thumb briskly over the tinder wheel to spark a flame. Once the paraffin cube had caught, he reached for the wooden bellows and poked the nozzle in. He kept working the bellows, watching the smoulders glow, the flames stretch and flutter on the gusts. He put too much strength into it, so that each time the bellows inhaled they filled with ash particles that then got expelled in puffs from the wire-gauze vent: after a few minutes the room was cloudy with ash; I could taste the dryness on my tongue. Rich brought the fire to beacon strength before laying the bellows down and leaning back to admire his handiwork. Then he walked to the green seat on castors in the corner and got his pipe out, and soon thick scarves of pipe smoke were swirling through the ash cloud, a mixed fog hanging in the yellow light of the drawing room.

Leeds have played that afternoon, and he's still bristling with excitement. Without warning, he makes a fist and punches the air with a stage-whisper 'Yes!', beaming, swelling with the team's success.

'The best team in the world,' he says. 'That's right, the best team in the world.' He smiles. 'Two-nil. Nothing could stop them!' He sits back, reflecting. 'Yes, it makes you proud.' He laughs to himself, shaking his head. 'It makes you *proud* to be a Leeds supporter.'

He carries the victory fervour with him from room to room: you can hear footstomps in the drawing-room floorboards, the stone spiral stairs shuddering as he thumps down them, beneath the light in its six-pointed star of black iron and glass, looking for me or our mother or father. It's not that he wants to engage in conversation, he just needs some other person to witness his exultation, the triumph shimmer coming off him; his investment is so complete, corporeal, it's as if he himself had led the team out at Elland Road that afternoon, decked in blue and gold. He picks up a commentator's phrase and repeats it, turning it over, relishing the feel of it in his mouth: 'Leeds *pulverized* Villa this afternoon. Yes, that's right, we *pulverized* them. *Pulverized*, that's the word.' He runs onto the front lawn and leaps in goal-celebration, punching the air again, rooks lifting from tree canopies as if people were shaking them out of their hair. Pounding back into the drawing room, he lights his pipe, leans back in the green chair and exhales, replete, entirely satisfied.

He kept the angle-flame Zippo in his trouser pocket, quick on the draw when candles appeared. There was a store of candles in a cupboard by the boiler room – striped birth-day candles, red and white candles with long wax drools down the sides, candles in tin and glass lanterns – and when the power failed on winter evenings one of us had to fetch and light them. I squabbled with Richard over this, because I wanted the pleasure of striking matches and Rich wanted the role his Zippo equipped him for, conjuring a light before anyone had thought to ask. At Christmas Mum planted holly in the plum pudding and poured warm brandy over it, and Rich was there straightaway, holding his Zippo against the pudding, a blue flame ghosting through the holly sprigs. Once, the lighter short on fuel, he produced a book of matches. He tore a match off and struck it. The whole strip caught fire, and for a moment he stood motionless with this dense white flare in his fingers, as if he were holding a new star in his hands.

o

The corollary of Richard's triumph shimmer was the despondency he sank into whenever Leeds lost. Then it was as if his inner world had gone dark, as if the day itself had crossed him in ways that allowed for no redress. Unable to settle, he carried the gloom from one room to another, frowning intently, rehearsing the wrong in a low voice addressed to no one in particular.

'What is it?' my mother asked.

'I'm just feeling rather *downput*,' Rich replied.

Downput: his special melancholy had a name.

One afternoon, we were going for a walk. Rich was in two minds. He stood on the square of flagstones outside the door and looked up, inspecting the sky; he peered into vague distances to left and right, a sea captain walking onto shore first thing to gauge the atmosphere, to judge the likelihood of a storm; he scrutinized the air for giveaway tints. The clouds were thick and low; all day, wet and dry spells had taken turns like chess players.

'Are you coming, Rich?' my mother asked.

'I'm not sure,' he said, frowning. 'The weather's making heavy weather of itself.'

The frown dissolved; Richard smiled, delighting in the words. My mother smiled back at him. He said it again, beaming: 'The weather's making heavy weather of itself!'

Mum and Dad encouraged him to read. He'd manoeuvre the green chair underneath the corner lamp and open the adventure story or footballer's biography so we heard the spine cracking. He didn't read so much as contemplate the pages, as if they could be absorbed passively, just by looking; he put the book down in his lap after a few minutes and got involved in fiddly pipe routines, rapping the earthenware bowl as if bringing a court to order, sparking the Zippo, his deep, wheezy in-breaths dragging oxygen through the smoulder. The first exhalation was the exaggerated performance of someone blowing out birthday candles, and when he puffed his cheeks and directed a cone of thick smoke at the ceiling he looked like Aeolus, god of winds, depicted in the blank ocean spaces of old maps; he'd tilt his head and watch the smoke hover in drifts and scarves, lamplight catching the edges; he'd think aloud, going over that afternoon's Leeds game, repeating a joke from a James Bond film, the book in his lap already forgotten.

He had a pile of Tintins on his bedside table, dog-eared hardcover editions with torn bindings, loose pages filed in haphazard order. His concentration didn't have stamina for other books. But he loved words. Puns, coinages and other verbal games were sources of delight, inexhaustible. He remembered a polished baby moon. The cafe was a palace of knives. 'My heart went sunk,' he said, after the plane took off. 'Didn't yours?'

Mum, especially, was his accomplice in such things. A word would give them pause and together they'd tease out the pun in it, passing it from one to another with embellishments and tweaks of emphasis. She was standing at the kitchen sink; Rich walked to her across the green linoleum, paused close behind and placed his right hand on her left shoulder.

'Mum,' he says, leaning close to her ear. 'Mum.'

He doesn't need to say that to get her attention: the Bible weight of his hand has already announced him.

'Shall I tell you something? Mum?'

'Yes?'

'You were saying, about the car. I was just thinking of something.'

'What was it?'

'The day is starting the ignition of life.'

She turned to face him.

'Yes,' he said, smiling. 'The day is starting the ignition of life.'

o

In December 1848, the *Boston Medical and Surgical Journal* published a letter from a doctor in Vermont named John Harlow. On September 13th, Harlow wrote, Phineas Gage, the twenty-five-year-old foreman of a crew working on the Rutland and Burlington Railroad, had been preparing a rock for blasting by filling a hole with explosive powder. Gage had been tamping the powder with an iron bar more than three feet long, pointed at one end and 'rendered comparatively smooth by use', when he happened to look round at men loading rocks onto a platform car behind him. In this lapse of attention, the bar had struck a spark off the rock, and the powder had exploded.

The tamping iron shot point-first through Gage's head, entering at his left cheek and 'taking a direction upward and backward' through his skull, throwing him to the ground. The foreman, witnesses reported, 'gave a few convulsive motions of the extremities, but spoke in a few minutes.' His men carried him to the road and took him back to Cavendish in an ox cart: he sat upright, and got out of the cart with little assistance. The tamping iron, meanwhile, had been found 'some rods distant, smeared with brain.'

Harlow examined, cleaned and dressed the wound. He describes 'an irregular oblong opening in the skull of two by three and one half inches' and notes that 'the pulsations of the brain were distinctly seen and felt.' He was able to insert his right index finger 'its entire length' into the opening in the skull, and his left index finger 'in like manner' into the wound in Gage's cheek. The patient 'bore his sufferings with heroic firmness' – the man and his bed 'were literally one gore of blood' – but still his 'sensorial powers' remained 'as yet unimpaired'. Gage insisted that he didn't want to see his friends, as he was going to be back at work in a day or two. He did improve, but not as quickly as he'd supposed: on November 25th, Gage returned to his home in Lebanon, New Hampshire.

In 1868, Harlow delivered a second report about Phineas Gage to the Massachusetts Medical Society. Gage had received his injury in September; the following April, Harlow recorded his health as 'good'. The opening in Gage's skull 'was entirely closed', and the doctor was 'inclined to say' that he had recovered. But Gage had changed. He had become 'fitful, irreverent, indulging at times in the grossest profanity, manifesting but little deference for his fellows, impatient of restraint or advice when it conflicts with his desires, at times pertinaciously obstinate, yet capricious and vacillating.' He'd applied for his old job, but his contractors, 'who regarded him as the most efficient and capable fore-man in their employ previous to his injury, considered the change in his mind so marked that they could not give him his place again. The equilibrium or balance, so to speak, between his intellectual faculties and animal propensities, seems to have been destroyed.' Gage, Harlow went on, had become 'a child in his intellectual capacity and manifestations'. The foreman, according to his friends, was 'no longer Gage'.

Denied his old job, Phineas Gage began to travel. He took the tamping iron with him: Harlow calls it his 'constant companion during the remainder of his life.' He spent almost eight years in Chile, looking after coach horses around Valparaiso and Santiago, before sailing north again to California. In February 1861, he began to have seizures. Gage died in May, twelve and a half years after his injury; post-mortem examination revealed the iron's damage to his brain, especially to the frontal lobes, the area of the cerebral cortex immediately behind the forehead. The accident, Harlow wrote, 'produced serious lesion of the brain substance – the anterior and middle left lobes of the cerebrum – disintegrating and pulpifying it.'

o

Richard could swing from gentle benevolence to aggression and back again within a few hours, as if a different personality had taken him over and then given ground. I didn't understand that his difficult behaviour, his bloody-mindedness, weren't intentional, the way my moods and actions were – that lesions in his frontal lobes were interfering with his capacity to think ahead or imagine himself into other people's shoes. When he was difficult, I blamed him for being difficult. I made him responsible.

Often the whole character of the day hung on the result at Elland Road. Before kick-off, Rich paced from room to room in a fury of anticipation. He held his portable radio against his ear, seizing on injury updates and pitch reports, repeating them aloud to himself, emphasizing certain phrases – 'Bremner's at the top of his game. He's at the top of his game. That's right, the *top of his game*' – his face breaking into a broad smile. He shook his head in happy disbelief.

He laid his right hand on Dad's shoulder.

'You'll be pleased to hear, Fa, that Eddie Gray's starting. Yes, he's back from injury. Eddie Gray, the winger.'

'Good,' Dad said. 'That's a good sign.'

Rich went outside, as if his excitement needed a more open range. He walked out onto the lawn and punched the air, celebrating. 'Good old Eddie! I knew you wouldn't let us down!' He kicked a dandelion with a full penalty-spot follow-through, then came back into the house, pulling the door behind him with a slam, pounding up the stone spiral stairs to check the TV.

'It's lunchtime, Rich,' Dad said.

'I don't care about that,' Richard answered. He didn't look up. He sat on the front edge of the chair, tilting it forward, elbows on his knees, chin resting on his hands. 'The only thing I care about right now is Leeds.'

'Lunch is ready, Rich,' I said, seeing an opportunity to wield power, to give him orders despite his seniority.

'I'm not worried.' He rocked the chair on its slender front legs.

We became Leeds supporters by proxy. If the team lost, Richard sank into despair, an inarticulate rage he carried from room to room, a thundercloud expression on his face, all the springs and coils wound tighter in him. He sat through meals in silence. He helped himself to enormous, heaped portions, as much as the plate could hold, then dropped the plate onto the mat as if testing it for cracks, food spilling off the heap onto the table. He didn't start eating straightaway but took a deep breath and expelled it with deliberate force, a release of pressure, smoker's wheeziness giving body and detail to the exhalation. Then he leaned back on the chair, making the joints wince, using his knees under the table ledge to prevent him tipping. No one said anything. We could all hear the wooden chair protest beneath him. He heard it too and leaned back further to increase the strain.

'I'm not sure that's very good for the chair, Rich,' Dad said.

'Who asked for your opinion?'

The chair winced again as he spread his shoulders and stretched away from the table.

'Was the heron there this morning?' my mother asked.

But Richard was set on his course and wouldn't be diverted.

'You should keep you mouth shut,' he said, still fixed on Dad's intervention. He looked straight ahead, or down at his food. 'Don't speak until you're spoken to.'

I didn't say anything. The room's fibres stiffened; the

threat of violence sharpened the air. Something mean deep inside me savoured the tension. I found it exciting to be on this knife edge, only the slightest provocation needed to set off a storm.

'Remember what we said, about behaviour,' my mother said.

'You keep out of it.'

'That's enough, Rich,' Dad said.

'Shut your mouth.'

'No, don't talk like that.'

'Are you deaf?' He turned to face my father. He raised his fork to Dad's neck.

'Keep your mouth shut or there'll be trouble,' he said.

He held the fork at Dad's Adam's apple, his whole body clenched. Dad leaned away, looking down at the table; Rich stretched his arm, keeping the fork prongs poked into Dad's neck. I didn't move. Rich lowered the fork and turned back to his plate. Dad got up and carried his plate and glass to the sink.

My parents had to show two groups of foreign students round the house that afternoon. Mum took me aside.

'It's best if you just keep out of his way,' she said.

I ignored her. I couldn't admit it, but I liked being in the vicinity of that pent-up rage, the day poised on the brink of violence. My outdoor haunts seemed safe, their solitude too cosy. I went in to watch TV with Richard. When I said there was a programme I liked on the other side, it was a way of raising the stakes. I wanted to test my power against his. I wanted to provoke his fury and show I could withstand it.

So I pushed my luck, telling him to turn the volume down, or change the channel, saying it was my turn, he'd already been watching for hours. He didn't say anything. He drummed his fingers on the edge of Mum's desk, piano hammers striking a repeated tattoo – dadada-*da*, dadada-*da*, dadada-*da* – that filled the room with martial foreboding, threatening in its intensity. Each repetition bore deeper into my repose. I pretended to ignore it, but the noise persisted, Richard's fingers going like pistons. The drumming was a challenge, to see how long I could hold out.

'Rich, please stop,' I said.

He stopped. I waited for his response to my intervention, either silence or a resumption of drumming, knowing that silence would only be provisional, an empty space into which drumming could at any time intrude.

'Who asked for your opinion?' he said.

'No one.'

'Well, then.'

The drumming started up again. Da-da-da-*da*. Da-da-da-*da*.

'You're not the only person who wants to watch the TV,' I said.

'I don't know what you're talking about.'

His fingers kept thudding into the desk.

'Please, Rich. It's very distracting.'

'I don't know what you're talking about.'

Now we heard the foreign students walking above us, down the Long Gallery, conversation hubbub seeping through the floorboards.

'Keep it down!' Rich shouted at the ceiling.

The plaster shook as the last students walked over.

'Stupid idiots,' he said, turning back to the TV.

Our private side was an inner life, the part of the house hidden from general view. The foreign students walked above us down the Long Gallery while I fought with my brother. I didn't understand then that his persistence and rigidity of thinking were consequences of his brain damage and couldn't be dissolved by argument. My reasoning didn't get me anywhere. Rich leaned over and rapped me on the skull with the knuckles; he flicked me on the temple to end the discussion.

'How about a nice walk, Rich,' Dad suggested.

'What would I want to do that for?' he answered, not looking up.

We came back to find him asleep on the sofa, TV blaring.

o

The amateur dramatic society that performed *A Midsummer Night's Dream* on the back lawn had given my parents a new punt pole of limber varnished ash, a commemorative plaque screwed in and a two-pronged steel fork at the tip. Too heavy for me to carry, it lived in the Old Kitchens with the

green boat's oars and rowlocks, the red-and-white-striped
life-ring and the orange life-vest whose chunky black zip was
the first I could fit and draw up unassisted. The punt lived
here too, resting on its side. You needed four to carry it
through the Ladies' Garden arch and slide it off the bank
into the water. Martin and Richard took turns with the
pole. Rich put all his strength into it: he was in a hurry;
he didn't know you had to let the pole linger in the water as
a rudder after you'd pushed off; the punt turned in comic
circles until he got the knack of it, water slapping beneath
us as we picked up speed. I sat at the prow and looked back
at Rich, in jeans and buttoned-up short-sleeved shirt and
Leeds United sunhat, a big digital watch strapped too tight
round his wrist. His bare feet are white, black hairs sprouting from the toes. The pole gives him gondolier distinction:
he's proud to be the source of power; he pushes down
with such insistence the fork gets stuck in the moat bed; he
wrestles it free and shoves again, the punt proceeding in
lurches towards the bridge.

The bridge arches seem too low to pass through but I
know it's possible: you just have to lie flat in the punt, keeping your head down, and once the prow's in position you
can pull yourself under, careful not to inhale mortar flecks
and spiders, plosions of stone dust released by hands scuff-
ing the brickwork. The craft slides into a tunnel four or five
yards long, and for a few seconds we're in a world of ripple
shimmer and spleenwort, cobwebs slung like hammocks

inches from our faces, the punt's edges scraping the arch before we emerge again, light and acoustics back to normal, Rich resuming his gondolier stance to shunt us on.

The water warmed up through July; my mother and sister were usually the first to brave it. Even after weeks of high summer the heat never penetrated more than a couple of feet, which meant a thin quilt of warm water over icy depths, and a premium on swimming as flat as you could, keeping to that upper warmth. Below it lay another medium altogether, a dark understorey of mud, stone and weed; treading water stirred the lower cold up into the warmth, glacial streaks and swirls sliding like eels across your skin. The first swimmer had the best of it: everyone else found the surface's clement bath temperature already compromised by cold kicked up from the deep. The warm layer felt thick and velvety, the brown-green water floated with drifts of duck sewage and leaf mould, and sometimes you swam among reflections of trees, the park's oaks trembling as your stroke pushed ripples through them. I was frightened of the tangle-danger of drifting algae clumps, the sensation of weed dragging across my feet, the soft, silty bottom substance. I thought about carnivorous pike patrolling the depths; I knew sharks were attracted to splashing swimmers, so I tried to swim without disturbing the water; the twins had seen *Jaws* and teased me with the menacing two-note music. I remembered pike I'd caught and killed, and imagined their brothers gathering for revenge, my toes suddenly vulnerable, the first bite's downward yank coming any second.

Mum appeared in her bathing suit; she pushed stray curls of hair under a plastic bathing cap covered with frilly flower decorations; she lowered herself in slowly off the grass bank by the Ladies' Garden arch. Dad hardly ever swam, but when he did I saw his bony white legs kicking in the murk, his head raised like a turtle's above the water. To swim a whole moat circuit was to move among moorhens, coots and mallards, dragonflies and damselflies, lily pads sitting on the water like jam papers, a heron standing up to its ankles in the shallows: through the cool, shadowed north-east corner, past the sluice-gate jungle of bamboo and elephant rhubarb, down the open straight between the lawn and rising parkland and under the ripple-lit bridge arch where small splash-sounds were amplified and your breathing echoed.

I dreamed of sailing on the moat. I imagined how I'd have to stand out on the rails to keep the boat on an even keel when the wind got up; I saw myself tacking to make headway against the wind, or screaming on a reach past the park's oaks, only the bridge preventing complete circum-navigations of the island. Mum folded a dust sheet in half on the diagonal and rigged this triangular mainsail to a window pole; we launched the green boat together and I sat in the stern holding the sail's loose corner while Mum sat amidships clamping the mast between her knees. The boat drifted; the sail flapped disconsolately while I paddled us through the drag of a lily patch; I picked up my corner again and pulled the sail tight against the mast. We both saw it fill with wind – not just saw but felt it too, a tug in the hands, the sheet's creases vanishing into a taut, smooth curve. I held onto the sheet corner with both hands, Mum held tight to the mast, and we began to move, powered by wind. You could hear water underneath the boat and see wind spilling off the hypotenuse, but then the sheet pulled free from its knot at the mast-top and we slowed again. Mum gathered it up and secured it once more to the end of the window pole, but it was too late: the wind had dwindled, we just had the memory of that brief, euphoric surge, a few seconds in which we'd got what we wanted from the elements by intelligent collaboration, in which I didn't think about how much I wanted a sailing boat, I was absorbed in our forward motion, the swollen tension of our sail, water slapping beneath us like applause.

o

Rich rode a racing bike, tape coming loose on the dipped handlebars. The gravel drive round the lawn between castle and stables made a racetrack on which laps could be notched up and record times broken. He cycled with reckless, headlong intensity, back wheels skidding in the gravel at each corner; when he crossed a cattle grid you felt the tremor in your own bones. No matter how fast he was going, he'd stop by clutching both brakes as hard as he could, wheels carving through the loose stones with a sound like a sail ripping. One side of the square ran directly at the door we used as our front door: two big panes of glass in a cream-painted wooden frame. When you walked or bicycled towards it the glass showed your reflection approaching, so that each time I ran back to the house I saw myself running out to meet me. We didn't know if Rich suffered a partial seizure on the bike and just went blank, or whether the kinetic thrill of the laps – each one faster than the one before – had gone to his head, but one afternoon he forgot to slow down and turn the corner on that home straight, and he crashed through the glass door, lying concussed in the window debris with his mangled bike on top of him.

He had trouble getting started. Once started, he had trouble stopping. I'd got a Scalextric set for my birthday, two plastic throttles to control the cars. I laid the black track on the carpet in a figure of eight and knelt beside it for hours, mastering the technique, squeezing the trigger to accelerate down the straights or swing cars round the banked curve, learning to slow down as the cars approached the flat bends and skid chicanes, getting a feel for how the cars responded to the trigger, how they took their cue from whatever electric current I released into the steel contact rails.

Rich wanted to play with it too.

'I don't know if I'll be very good at this,' he said. 'You'll be much better at it than me, I should imagine.'

We knelt beside the starting grid with the red and yellow throttles held out in front of our chests.

'Come on then, Niki Lauda,' Rich said. 'Or should I say Alain Prost? I don't think I stand much of a chance against you, Alain Prost!'

My car sped off the starting line. But Rich couldn't get

the hang of it; he couldn't judge the pressure on the trigger. Either he didn't squeeze enough and his car sat on the grid emitting a low electric buzz, or he squeezed too hard, holding the trigger tight against the handle, his car flipping off crash barriers, flying off banked curves, smashing into pieces on the radiator. Sometimes his car slewed perpendicular to the track, the guide blade like a boat's daggerboard still in the groove of the contact rails, the wire braid plates still picking up current, but the back wheels spinning vainly, getting no traction. The wheels screamed as Rich kept squeezing the throttle, a burning electric smell rising off the track as I completed lap after lap, passing my brother's stranded car at speed, without effort.

'Stupid thing,' he said, frowning at the red plastic throttle in his hand. 'I don't know what's wrong with it.' He released the trigger and squeezed it again: the wheels whined on open air. 'Blasted thing,' he said. He picked his car off the track and inspected it all over, examining the chassis for evidence of sabotage.

We swapped cars and throttles. But still I cruised round the circuit, lapping Richard repeatedly as he spun off and struggled to fit the guide blade back between the rails. Sometimes I slowed down on purpose, allowing him to get ahead and keep a lead, only to accelerate past him on the last banked corner and coast victorious through the chequered flag.

Doctors at the centre referred to his 'executive dysfunction'; they described the frontal lobes as the 'executive' area of the brain: conductor of the orchestra, CEO of the company. I knew my brother wasn't like other people, and I was starting to understand that this was because there were scars in his brain, behind his forehead. But I couldn't think of Richard's personality as a set of symptoms; I couldn't think of his character as a manifestation of disease. That would have implied the existence of an ideal healthy Richard my brother was an imperfection of, a dream-Richard this actual person couldn't measure up against. But there wasn't any other Richard.

He turned taps off so tightly it was hard for the rest of us to open them again; after a bath or shave he wound the plug-chain round the tap's neck as if to garrotte it; sometimes he tied the chain off with a knot round the tap as if he were mooring the whole bath to a wharf bollard. He wrapped Christmas and birthday presents in several layers and trussed them from one end to the other like bodies made ready for burial at sea: it took minutes to open those presents (sometimes you needed to fetch scissors) and when the object itself at last appeared Rich would be standing beside you, his hand like an epaulette on your shoulder, smiling expectantly, anxious that what he'd chosen met with your approval, perhaps even revealing what he'd paid for it, how he'd picked up the Brut aftershave at the centre's bring-and-buy sale: 'I shouldn't tell you, really, I know, but I bet you can't guess how much it cost. Come on, have a go, have a guess!' The thoroughness with which he strait-jacketed those presents was the same thoroughness he brought to sealing envelopes or applying a plaster to a knife cut on his finger – nothing left to chance, the plaster drawn tight like a tourniquet, the ends pressed down until long after the adhesive had dried, then pressed again just to make sure, his mouth open in concentration, his tongue pushing unconsciously in his cheek.

He hadn't washed or changed his clothes for a week.

'How about a nice bath?' Mum suggested.

Richard was watching the television.

'What do you mean?' he said. He kept his eyes on the TV.

'Wouldn't a bath be nice?'

'I don't know what you're talking about.'

'It just seems quite a while since you last had one.'

'You should mind your own business.'

'Wouldn't you like to feel all clean and fresh?'

'You should keep out of it.'

Mum looked out of the arched window. The crow was standing on the lawn in front of the stables.

'I'm just suggesting it,' she went on. 'How about a nice hot bath?'

'It's all right, I'm not deaf.'

'I wasn't sure you heard me. I want you to have a bath.'

'I don't have to.'

'No, you don't.'

'You can't make me.'

'I can't.'

'You should mind your own business.'

'Don't be like that.'

'I don't know what you're talking about.'

'All right,' Mum said. She glanced at the television. 'We'll talk about it later, when this is finished.'

Rich leaned forward, making the chair joints squeak. 'I don't know what you're talking about,' he said.

o

In April 1861, shortly before Phineas Gage died in California, the surgeon Paul Broca began treating a fifty-one-year-old man with a gangrenous right leg at the Bicêtre Hospital in Paris. The patient, named Leborgne, had suffered from epilepsy since childhood, was paralysed down the right side of his body, and hadn't been able to speak for twenty years. He was nicknamed 'Tan' – the sound he made when he tried to give his name. 'The state of his intelligence,' Broca would report, 'could not be exactly determined': the surgeon was convinced his patient 'understood almost all that was said to him, but he had only gesticulations of his left hand available for issuing information.' Leborgne answered every question with the words 'tan, tan', along with a variety of gestures, 'quite successful in rendering most of his thoughts.' Broca found that the most useful questions were those Tan could answer with numbers: 'he gave them by opening or closing his fingers.'

Tan died within a week. When Broca examined his brain he found extensive damage to the frontal lobes, especially 'a chronic and progressive softening' centred in the third frontal convolution of the left hemisphere.

In October, Broca saw another case of speechlessness, an eighty-three-year-old man named Lelong. After fracturing his neck in a fall, Lelong was brought to Broca as a surgical patient. He seemed normal in almost all respects, but he could only say five words: 'Lelo' (for his own name), 'oui', 'non', 'tois' (for 'trois') and 'toujours'. Lelong died twelve days after he met the surgeon, and on post-mortem examination Broca found a brain lesion on the left side of the frontal lobes, in exactly the same place as Leborgne's.

By April 1863, Broca was able to speak in detail about eight cases of speech loss or *aphasia*. The brains of all eight patients showed lesions in the same area of the left hemisphere, and Broca proposed the existence of a centre for articulate language in the frontal lobes, as Fritsch and Hitzig had proposed a motor centre.

More than a century before, Emanuel Swedenborg had suggested that different parts of the brain had different functions, and had attributed particular intellectual activity to the frontal lobes: 'If this portion of the cerebrum therefore is wounded,' he wrote in 1741, 'then the internal senses – imagination, memory, thought – suffer; the very will is weakened, and the power of its determination blunted.' Now Broca too suggested that the frontal lobes served such functions as judgement and reflection.

In Yorkshire, David Ferrier damaged the frontal lobes of three monkeys. His subjects showed no motor or sensory symptoms, but Ferrier thought he 'could perceive a very decided alteration in the animal's character and behaviour

. . . Instead of, as before, being actively interested in their surroundings, and curiously prying into all that came within the field of their observation, they remained apathetic, or dull, and dozed off to sleep, responding only to the sensations and impressions of the moment, or varying their listlessness with restless and purposeless wanderings to and fro. While not actually deprived of intelligence, they had lost, to all appearance, the faculty of attentive and intelligent observation.' Ferrier believed that these animals were suffering from disorders of attention. 'Removal of the frontal lobes,' he concluded, 'causes no motor paralysis, or other evident physiological effects, but causes a form of mental degradation, which may be reduced in ultimate analysis to loss of the faculty of attention.'

Since the nineteenth century, studies of patients with head injuries and tumours, and of patients after surgical removal of frontal lesions, have shown that damage to the frontal lobes tends to result in the same set of cognitive and behavioural characteristics: a lack of initiative and spontaneity; low alertness; difficulty in sustaining attention; difficulty in planning ahead; sluggishness of responses; lack of normal adult tact. The frontal-lobe patient often has difficulty in initiating and organizing new behaviour, and shows a diminished appreciation of how their behaviour affects others. The patient can cope with familiar routines, but struggles to develop new behaviour based on deliberation and choice. He or she may show a blunting of emotional responses, as well as emotional 'lability': their mood can shift rapidly on little provocation. They may show impaired control of aggressive behaviour, leading, in some cases, to outbursts of violence.

○

The life of the house went on. Guides arrived to slide the heavy brass bolts on the Great Hall's inner and outer doors and welcome groups of visitors – fine arts and historical societies, Women's Institute coach parties, gardening clubs, foreign students on whirlwind Cotswold tours. Almost every day I watched a crowd of strangers pass under the gatehouse and pause to photograph the castle's ironstone front and top-splendour of chimneys before funnelling into the Great Hall. The guides – Mrs Parrington, Mrs Spring, Mrs Pelham-Lane, Mrs Curtis, Mrs Cozens – were recurring faces in the parade that streamed through the house: along the Groined Passage and Long Gallery, through the Great Parlour and Council Chamber, down the west stairs into the Oak Room, leaving by the door concealed in the oak panelling, stepping out into the Ladies' Garden with its four clipped hawthorns and babble of roses. I stood in the kitchen with my ear at the secret door into the Dining Room, eavesdropping on the guide's brief histories and the tourists' questions.

Weekday mornings Dad left for work at the chartered surveyor's office he'd set up with his friend George Laws. He wore an old tweed jacket, elbows reinforced with pieces of leather the same size and shape as the panels you punched from Kleenex boxes to get at the tissues, walking briskly with a short-strided gait up the drive towards the gatehouse arch, a batch of manila folders under one arm, free hand in the pocket of his grey flannel or tan corduroy trousers, wale worn thin at the knees. He had an office at home too, a cold, bare room off the west stairs with a simple bar heater and a map of the estate hanging on the wall behind his desk, features of the castle – Gateway Tower, Embattled Wall, Spring – marked on it, the Sor Brook coloured blue, Yeats's poem 'He Wishes for the Cloths of Heaven' copied onto a postcard and stuck in one of the map's blank field-spaces beyond the park.

He disappeared up there for hours to see to the estate, go over the accounts, respond to enquiries and requests. He wrote letters at an old bureau in the library off the drawing room, a hinged writing surface inset with a square of green cloth, an interior of slim drawers and cubbyholes, a bottle of blue Quink in the right-hand corner, while Mum worked at a heavy Victorian pedestal desk heaped with papers next to it, facing the arched medieval window and the white door that led into the chapel, a standard lamp between them. She wrote notes about Richard's most recent visit, preparing for a conference with his psychologist, looking up to ask Dad whether Rich woke at two or three in the afternoon on Saturday, and what it was he'd said when he came round from a seizure. Dad had a list of all the roses in the garden, and he was writing their names on flat metal tags, each threaded with a finger-length of wire for twisting round thorned main stems.

Most winters he wrote down the names of roses – 'Buff Beauty', 'Bobby James', 'Fantin Latour', the metal badges spread on his desk like medals. Later, he'd find a spot on each rose to fix the tag, somewhere the metal badge wouldn't draw attention to itself, wouldn't ask to be looked at before the rose itself was looked at. Garden enthusiasts strolled the borders all summer, and if I saw them pause at a rose and wonder what it was called, I'd step between them and point out the identifying brooch, my father's handwriting among the leaves: 'Fritz Nobis', 'Marguerite Hilling', 'Ena Harkness', 'New Dawn'.

Bert steered the Dennis across the lawns. He fixed eyelets into mortar and strung wire between them to help the climbers. He stood over a wasps' nest in the west lawn and ran to the shed in the stables before taking his trousers down to pull out the stings. He clipped box hedges with old lopping shears and trimmed the yew to a sculptural curve between the gatehouse and stables, his ladder sinking slightly before twigs and branches took the strain. He set up tripod sprinklers in the Ladies' Garden and I watched long ropes of moat water pulse from them as if each sprinkler were throwing a lasso again and again over the roses.

Dad had a black leather note-holder, stapled on one side where the stitching had come loose; he cut old invitations and compliments slips to size and fitted them in the corner slits. When we visited other gardens he drew the note-holder from his inside jacket pocket and wrote down the names of plants. I got impatient when he and my mother discussed with gardeners the soil and light requirements of particular shrubs and perennials. I tugged on my mother's sleeve as if on a bell-pull: I wanted to keep sounding the note of my presence in her head; I wanted an ice cream; I wanted to be home in time for *Doctor Who*; I felt excluded by the adult gibberish of botanical names and opted for boredom instead of curiosity in response.

I was nine when Dad pointed to a small plant at the front of the Battlement Border and said the words 'Alchemilla mollis'. I'd heard him use botanical names before but this was the first time he'd yoked the strange words so deliberately to a thing. He got me to say the words after him: *Alchemilla mollis*. At first I couldn't get them right. The words knotted and snarled in my mouth; we had to work through them syllable by syllable, the names a technique my lips and tongue needed to master by practice. But as soon as I said them once, it was easy. *Alchemilla mollis. Alchemilla mollis.* I looked down at the plant, leaf rims crimped in pleats, the small yellow-green flowers, and said the plant's own name back to it as if in greeting. The words slid fluently, a musical pleasure in that procession of l's and m's, the see-saw rhythm of *Alchemilla mollis.* As soon as I had its name in my head I started to notice the plant all over the garden: at the front of borders, seeded in cracks between flagstones. The name was a kind of recognition. Now *Alchemilla mollis* stood out from other, anonymous plants.

o

Rich was telling Joyce, Mrs Upton and Mrs Green about imminent Leeds United fixtures, showing off his new velveteen Leeds United slippers.

'Are you having a drop of coffee, then, Richard?' Joyce asks.

'I wouldn't say no.'

'And what mug are you going to have it in?'

'I should think you know the answer to that, Joyce,' he says, smiling. He reaches for the Leeds United mug hanging from a hook below the cupboards, and holds it up so the blue and gold shield catches the light. 'There's only one mug I can drink from. There's only one mug for a Leeds United supporter.'

'Good old Leeds,' Joyce says.

'Yes,' Rich continues, dreamily. 'It's got to be Leeds. It's got to be Leeds United, every time.'

He stares at the blue and gold shield in a trance of pride.

'Do you know something, Joyce?' he says, looking up.

'What's that, Richard?'

'Your little dog, she licked my cheeks, she was so happy to see me. She painted my face with dog kisses.'

'Sweet little thing!' Joyce says, laughing.

'She did! She painted my face all over with dog kisses!'

I was just hanging around. The twins were at university; Dad was at work in the office beyond the kitchen gardens, or meeting landowners, farmers and tenants; Mum was showing groups of students and tourists round the house, or arranging flowers in the Great Hall and Oak Room vases, or rubbing oil and wax into books, floorboards and armour. I played nonsense chords on the piano and loitered in the kitchen with Joyce, Mrs Upton, Mrs Green and Mrs Dancer, but by lunchtime they'd have disappeared through the gatehouse arch, back into their lives on the far side of the moat, and if Bert didn't have a job for me and I was bored of being on my own I'd look for Richard.

Sometimes I'd find him in a small room off the west stairs, a few steps down into a bedlam of rolled-up rugs and decrepit fishing rods, a carpenter's workbench with screws and clips in the backboard to carry tools. Rich had used a black marker to trace the tools like bodies at crime scenes – hammer, drill, awl, screwdriver and tenon saw outlined on the wood, a name above each shape in my brother's rounded handwriting. The workbench had an iron vice, and now I watched Rich fit a piece of scrap wood between the clamps and turn the shiny bar to close them up. Even after the wood was tightly held he put all his strength into it, forcing the bar round another inch or two, holding his breath, reddening with exertion. The wood seemed to be getting smaller between the clamps, and when he forced the bar again the whole bench shifted on the floorboards, the awl dropping from its fixture and chinking in a box of nails.

'Blast!'

He didn't know his own strength. He liked to pull the handbrake on when Mum parked the Dormobile. He'd yank it up and keep pulling, beyond the highest ratchet, as if he was trying to leave the brake secured on a tooth no one had thought to install, and then he'd put both hands to it and pull again as if to tear the whole thing up by the roots. We went in the boat with Dad: I jumped out as soon as we touched land; Rich stowed the oars and disembarked behind me; he bent down and took hold of the boat's rim, and before Dad had even got to his feet Rich heaved the boat up and hauled it over the high bank, changing the boat's angle so rapidly that the stern with our father in it plunged into the water. Dad gripped both sides of the boat to stop himself from falling, but already he was drenched from the waist down.

Often, after he's been aggressive, he's overcome with a terrible remorse. 'I'm such a horrible person,' he says. 'I don't know how anyone could be friends with a person like me.' He has his hand on my mother's shoulder – a weight we could all identify more precisely than a stone or kilogramme – and he's leaning right in close against her ear, as if to be sure his apologies have struck home. And just as he won't be content until he's wound the plug-chain knot-tight round the bath tap, so he'll keep harping on his guilt, going over his regrets in arias of sorrow that try everyone's patience almost as much as the initial bad behaviour had. His lapses cause him as much distress as any of Leeds's bad performances, and it's a relief that his memory is so porous, the violences so quickly forgotten – each particular shame is hard enough for him to bear; the aggregate would be intolerable. Sometimes when I let people into the house – the doorbell linked by wire to a copper pull – I tell them my brother's at home and that he's got epilepsy. I'm still learning that epilepsy only means a tendency to have seizures, and that it's not Richard's epilepsy so much as brain damage and anti-convulsant drugs that make him the way he is, but it's my way of saying he's not like other people, my unsophisticated version of a warning I've heard my mother and father give, a way of preparing strangers so they'll slacken the strings of their expectations and not be caught off guard by Richard's unpredictable bolshiness or ingenuous warmth.

o

I fished for perch, roach, tench and pike; I rowed full moat circuits against the clock, breaking my own record times, fine-tuning the business of stowing the oars and rowlocks and lying flat on the deck boards so the boat could glide under one bridge arch or the other without stalling; I climbed trees in the park and lost myself in yellow Wisden cricket annuals and Commando war comics and scoured the Barracks for secret doors and passageways, pillaging chests for forgotten guns; I breathed humid nettle air in the tumbledown Victorian greenhouses and stepped further by degrees into the pitch darkness of the Old Kitchens; I sat at the Formica table with Mrs Upton, Mrs Dancer and Mrs

Green, or alongside Joyce, shelling peas and broad beans into dented colanders; I hoed the lawn edges with Bert and painted the garage doors and cemetery railings with Harry Bennett, and sometimes I walked on my own up the hill through the scrubby wasteland district of nettles and elder bushes and stood in front of Thomas's headstone, wondering what it would be like if he were here to ride a bike with me along the single-track road to Fulling Mill and Broughton Grounds.

Dad kept his jumpers neatly folded on the bottom three shelves of the dressing-room cupboard, two shelves of medicines, bandages, ointments and plasters above them, beyond my reach unless I stood on a chair or the upturned metal wastepaper basket – nowhere else in the house you'd encounter the word *linctus*, or pink calamine lotion and dark blue Milk of Magnesia bottles, syrup bottles sticky with drizzle. Richard was drawn to these shelves. Often, walking across the landing, I saw him standing at the white cupboard, rummaging through foil pill strips and flip-top boxes of assorted plasters.

'What are you looking for, Rich?' I asked.

The question was mean-spirited, an assertion of power – a way of reminding my brother I could report things to our parents; that, despite being so much younger, I was privy to the secrets of acceptable behaviour and Richard wasn't; I knew he shouldn't be taking pills without Mum or Dad saying he could; I lived with them in a country of undamaged brains from which he was forever excluded.

'Mind your own business,' he said, still browsing the tablets and lotions.

When Rich was home there were foil strips of pills on the shelf under the kitchen clock: phenobarbitone, phenytoin, diazepam, sodium valproate. He had a navy blue pill organizer with a sliding see-through lid, days of the week and times of day printed in black in the compartments, white pill-dust gathered in the corners, and by now he was a virtuoso of tablets and capsules: he didn't even need a glass of water, he just chucked them at the back of his throat and flicked his head to dispatch them down.

At midday or one o'clock Mum might send me upstairs to see if I could wake him. I carried the task with me like an executive power. I climbed the narrow stone stairs to the door decorated with Paninero stickers of Leeds United players and a plaque on which the words 'Richard's Room' were printed beside a Leeds United crest. The handle was blue-green and moulded in the shape of a heron's head and bill, and when you pressed down on the bill to open the door the heron seemed to nod its agreement that you should proceed inside.

I'd come up here exploring when Rich was at the epilepsy centre, rifling through drawers and boxes. His room had high windows, a chest of drawers between them with a reproduction Leeds United trophy on top, a metal ring hanging from the wall, threaded with ties: wool, silk, polyester, spotted, striped, paisley, Leeds blue and gold, clip-on bows for church at Easter and Christmas, a many-stranded thickness sprouting like a horse's tail from the ironstone. Rich kept his records in a wire rack on the left-hand window ledge (Richard Clayderman and James Galway albums, colliery band collections, live Gilbert and Sullivan recordings) and on the right-hand ledge was a silver turntable with a smoked perspex lid, burly headphones with padded ear cups, a needle that descended with stately restraint no matter how hard you flicked the lever.

I didn't try to wake him straightaway. I stood next to his bed, looking around. He's got an alarm clock, a hammer dinging between exterior bells, but the clangour doesn't make a dent in his unconsciousness. Side-effect drowsiness spreads through him like embalmer's fluid and seems to weigh him down; I have to prod him hard on the shoulder to make him stir – it's as if he's emerging not from a night's sleep but from a whole season's hibernation, each eyelid a stone he has to roll back from the mouth of a cave. 'Time to get up, Rich,' I say, prodding. 'Lunch is ready.' When finally he opens his eyes and lifts his head his face is set in a dark frown, the new day's world an affront he'll have to deal with against his will. Mostly the fits happen in the night. He sleeps through into the afternoon and comes downstairs subdued, dazed in the aftermath. The seizures seem to bludgeon him from the inside. Mum talks softly to him, asking if he'd like anything, something to eat or drink.

'What would you say to a nice mug of coffee? Milky coffee, would that be nice?'

'Please,' Rich answers. He hardly ever says 'Yes'. It's always 'Please'. Or, if he's perkier, 'I wouldn't say no.'

o

Contractors came to dredge the moat. Dad raised the sluice gate in the south-east corner, the water draining into the Sor Brook, gushing off the falls by Harry Bennett's. We breathed the wrack stench of newly exposed mud, dead fish and dried weed, sun glinting off white stones, china fragments and freshwater mussel shells strewn round the beach. A workman lost control of a loader on the bridge and crashed through the wall, jumping off in time to see the vehicle plunge nose-first into the moat-bed. A dredging crane with clanking, toothed jaws moved on caterpillar tracks round the banks, mud slops dropping as each full load swung over dry land. The crane left a mound of moat-spoil in the north-east corner, close to my tree house. We threw grass seed over it and a year later the slagheap was a green hummock backing into trees. For a while, I visited the mound every day. I was sure a supernatural power resided in it, a presence I ought to pay attention to, and I made a daily ritual of crossing the bridge and walking round the moat to this strange knoll, greeting it with gestures of humility and respect.

I didn't understand the power in that mound of earth deposited by the churchyard fence. I was only dreaming I got out of bed, crossed the landing to the top of the spiral stairs and looked down at creatures gathered on the rug below, half-human, half-toad, warty and glistening, but for months afterwards I checked the rug was empty before I went down. For a long time I kept away from the Barracks because of the Victorian tailor's dummy that stood among old leather trunks and pieces of furniture draped with dust-sheets. The dummy had a man's torso upholstered in faded red cloth – its head, neck and legs were unadorned pieces of wood, but still it was just human enough, standing upright among gables, looking as if it had been waiting for somebody for years. I wondered if I were the person it had been waiting for: I didn't want to go near it, in case it flinched, or bent towards me.

Once I went up into the Barracks and looked down the passage to the room at the far west end, expecting to see the dummy, framed in the doorway, under the cobwebbed sky-light. But it had gone. I spun round, thinking the dummy must be coming up behind me, but it wasn't there. I walked slowly down the passage towards the doorway, on full alert; I pressed my back against the side of the passage to look into the room from a safe angle. The dummy was in the corner, a few yards from its habitual position. I kept staring at it, breathing quickly; I had to be sure the dummy wasn't going to move.

Gargoyles jutting from the oldest corners of the house had the faces of griffins, winged lions, mouths held open in unending roars; corbel faces had the eerie permanence of death masks, as if there were actual people buried in the walls, only their faces protruding; enormous spiders roamed the pipework, emerging at night to spread themselves like starfish in the baths. I dreamed of intruders in the house. They had malign intent. I ran through the rooms, opening and closing doors. The intruders were almost upon me, but I knew shortcuts; I had every detail of the castle's labyrinth in my head; I knew if I just kept running I'd keep beyond the reach of my pursuers.

o

Rich was eleven years ahead of me but I was catching up. We both liked to hit a tennis ball against the span of open wall between the arched kitchen window and the buttress. We weren't worried that this wall was nearly seven hundred years old and flakes of ironstone fell off it each time our forehands thwacked the lichens. Sometimes our aim lapsed and the ball tocked on the kitchen window, Joyce looking up startled from the sink, a dustprint like a dab of face powder on the glass. We had a simple catching machine, a square of string netting fixed in a frame by elastic cords: propped at the right angle, the net flung a cricket ball back at you with whatever strength you'd thrown it. Sometimes Rich and I both wanted to use the catching net – sometimes I wanted to use it *because* he wanted to use it – and we'd squabble over whose turn it was, the way we'd argue over TV channels or who'd had more time at the tennis wall. He was more than twice my age, in his twenties by now, but we were peers in our enthusiasms, alike in that neither of us could operate independently in the world: we still looked to our parents for permissions and opportunities. But I was starting to recognize the gulf between us. I knew my childhood was a temporary predicament, and that as soon as I was old enough I'd be able to make my own way. I knew that autonomy was only a matter of time. But for Richard there was no such prospect of loosened constraints, no country of self-determination on the horizon. His childlikeness was indefinite. He was moated in.

o

Martin came home in his first car. I saw it slide through the gatehouse arch, an old Triumph Herald, navy blue, a convertible, the soft black roof folded open, my brother with one hand on the steering wheel, his right forearm resting on the door, the window wound down beneath it. He pulled up in front of the house, in shadow; I ran across the lawn to meet him. The Triumph was so much closer to a boy's scale than the Volkswagen camper van: small, compact, low to the ground, I could actually imagine myself driving it. The roof canvas was patched with gaffer tape; foam stuffing pushed through nicks and rips in the seat leather; wires hung loosely beneath the dashboard. Yet still this car was sleek and finned and blue, as if the sea had designed it.

'Get in,' my brother said.

He started the car again; we glided from shadow into August sunlight. The Triumph slipped through the gatehouse and crossed the moat, Mart accelerating as we reached the church and the drive swung us round into parkland, cattle grids rumbling as the Herald breezed across them. I let my forearm rest along the top of the door, tilting my face into the wind, the trees deep green explosions captured in freeze-frame, sheep braying from cool shade-rooms below the canopies. It's exhilarating to be moving so fast with nothing between us and the wind and light – a heady, kinetic rush, as if we're flying among trees and fields under our own power. My brother has one hand resting casually on the wheel, and now he seems to be piloting a speedboat across open water, a roadside hedge lifting like a wave alongside us, the Herald racing and veering off the surge.

Martin pointed to the pool of cassettes round my feet and told me to find *The River*. I passed it to him; he pushed it into a stereo secured beneath the dashboard by strips of yellow and red electrician's tape; he turned the music up until we could hear it over the engine and wind. The song was called 'Point Blank' and by the second chorus I'd picked up some of the words and yelled them out when Martin did, the air thick with pollen and wheat dust, the smell of elder bushes and nettles. We passed the Great Ground, the Woad Mill, the dairy buildings, the almshouses and Toll Cottage and cruised back into the park, trees immense around us, heavy with chlorophyll, fleece-thick, swollen like cumulus, the house's ironstone planes and angles edging from the green.

o

My friends' houses were warm, compact and efficient; other children, older and younger, played in gardens on both sides; there were toasted sandwiches, midnight feasts in bunk-beds, teenage sisters trying out lipstick, pop music on the radio. Julian wore a Siouxsie and the Banshees button badge on his denim jacket; Nick stole packs of cigarettes from his dad's sock drawer; Alex said he had five girlfriends. You could come down to breakfast in your pyjamas, Sean's mother floating round the kitchen in a loosely tied silk dressing gown cut like a jacket at her thighs. You could walk everywhere in bare feet without the shock of cold stone.

When school friends came to visit my house it didn't occur to me there was anything unusual about where I lived, anything that needed explaining. At first they'd be unsure how to react, how to move among exhibits, through uninhabited historical rooms, as if they had to recalibrate themselves to new scale and perspective. But the novelty of the old was persuasive, and soon they were rushing from one end of the house to the other, enthralled by spiral staircases, battlements, secret doors, swords you could pick up and wield two-handed, cannonballs you could test the weight of despite the laminated *Do Not Touch* signs propped around them. Their surprise and curiosity reminded me to be surprised and curious too, and it wasn't long before I was running ahead down the Long Gallery, china cups and plates trembling on the table-tops, or taking the West Stairs two at a time, one flight perpendicular to the next, a familiar headlong rhythm of footbeats on boards, or leading everyone outside to the iron cannon on rusting, spindly wheels, lighting an invisible fuse and mimicking the sizzle, hands clamped over my ears against the boom. But at night my friends' excitement gave way to trepidation: the enclosed darkness was too extensive; noises – creaking timbers, rattling windows, rogue winds buffeting through roofspaces and flues – had new, malevolent power; in the next room, suits of armour were stepping down off their stands and moving in a slow, wading gait towards the door.

'We don't have any ghosts,' my mother told groups of schoolchildren. 'Well, if we do, they're very *nice* ghosts, because they don't give us any trouble.'

This was the answer I gave when anyone asked me about ghosts. I didn't talk about what it was like to stand in front of the secret door and hear the rustling on the other side, or go down into the dank crypt darkness of the Old Kitchens. I couldn't explain how frightened I'd been in the Barracks when the tailor's dummy had left its station to wait for me in the gable shadows, or how the mound of moat-spoil contained a real presence to which I owed respect and duty. I didn't mention the Puritan preacher in the long black coat and broad-brimmed black hat that Mrs Upton, Mrs Green and Mrs Bennett had seen walking through mist across the bridge on separate occasions.

I wouldn't have been able to say what was ghost and what history. But I didn't like to loiter in the Long Gallery on my own. I'd run from Queen Anne's Room to the Great Parlour, portraits of ancestors flashing by on both sides, a flicker of wigs, ruffs, cloaks, slender wrists, medals, swords, dogs, gold braid and top hats. I came to know them piecemeal, hearing my mother and father point out one character or another: seventeenth-century William and Elizabeth, their ruffs detailed white gleams, wheels of light on their black shoulders; nineteenth-century Frederick, who'd told an architect working on the house that he wanted 'grand simplicity, without fandangling' (a phrase Dad held close to his heart, a motto); a soldier in the Royal Scots Fusiliers; a woman called Maria, playing the harp; a Regency buck who'd gone in for 'excesses of all kinds' and died from drinking too much champagne, leaving the house in such desperate condition that all its contents had been sold at auction in 1837.

The pictures frightened me when I was alone. I never paused in front of them or looked them directly in the eye. The portraits were a kind of haunting; they made me think of other people living in these rooms, centuries before, breathing the same stone and timber air, herons poised on the moatside, rooks and jackdaws milling round the flag. In broad daylight, Mum changing the flowers or painting the wallpaper, I'd glance at the pictures and look for familiar resemblances. But I didn't feel any connection to them as I ran up and down the Long Gallery. I was just a boy relishing the freedom of an enormous room, the empty track of carpet a runway on which I could reach take-off speeds. I wanted Dad to let me wind the grandfather clock by the Great Parlour door; I wanted Mum to let me water the rush matting in the Kings' Chamber, the chimneypiece a white relief sculpture showing girls dancing round an oak tree, hand in hand. A Latin inscription referred to Ovid's story of Erysicthon: the girls were dryads or wood nymphs; they wore toga-like robes that left arms, breasts and shoulders bare; the tree was the great oak in a grove sacred to Ceres, goddess of harvest and plenty. Erysicthon ordered his slaves to fell the tree, and when they hesitated he grabbed the axe himself and set to work, blood leaking from the cut bark. The sacred tree crashed down. The dryads asked Ceres to punish him; the goddess dispatched a nymph to the Scythian mountains to find Famine; Famine crept into Erysicthon's bed at night and breathed hunger into him. When he woke, his hunger was insatiable. He couldn't stop eating. He ate everything he could lay his hands on. He ate his own limbs.

o

Rich came home in high spirits, brimming with tenderness, beaming, greeting the ladies in the kitchen with bristly kisses, carrying his Leeds holdall up to his bedroom in bounds, two steps at a time, smiling at the Leeds players on the door, setting the holdall down carefully on the Leeds prayer mat. Spotting a heron from the window, he rushed downstairs again to fetch binoculars from the hall cupboard, concentrating as he closed the outer door behind him to avoid abrupt sounds that might startle the bird. The heron stood motionless on the far bank below my tree house, long yellow bill angled like a dagger at the water, but when Rich raised the binoculars to his face the heron launched itself upwards, flinging grey-white wings out from its body, each downstroke producing a perceptible surge of lift as if the heron were hoisting itself into the air by ropes and pulleys.

Neck retracted onto shoulders, the bird disappeared behind the stables. Rich held the binoculars close to his chest and walked across the lawn towards the gatehouse. He stopped and turned to me, index finger pressed to his lips. He pointed at the gatehouse and beckoned me to join him. I only needed a few steps before the angle was right and I could see straight through the arch to the bridge walls, the cattle grid by the church gate. The heron was standing on the left-hand wall, bony feet on the topstones. We walked towards it. The bird crouched and then leaped off the wall, flying west over the water towards the park, then turning south, disappearing behind the gatehouse and long, crenellated rampart.

Rich walked briskly to the end of the battlements and stepped out onto the open lawn. The heron had settled again on the far side, at the foot of the park, close to a tall hawthorn.

'There he is,' Rich said, lifting the binoculars. 'There he is.'

He was smiling, entirely satisfied. Sometimes he disappeared for an hour or more to follow a heron round the moat, coming back inside to report on the bird's whereabouts.

'Do you realize,' he asked, 'I actually saw him catch a fish.'

He had his hand on my mother's shoulder.

'I actually *saw* him,' he repeated. 'Through the binoculars. I must be very lucky. He's still there, I should think, if you want to see him, Mum. He's in the corner, by the brook. Yes, I think I must be *very* lucky.'

He loved an old board game called L'Attaque. Our set was falling apart, so he made a new board by cutting a square of stiff card, ruling a grid across it in felt tip and colouring the squares green and blue to indicate land and water. I watched him play with my father, Dad leaning forward from his armchair, Rich kneeling on the worn patch of yellow carpet in front of the fire. I watched as they deployed armies, positioning sappers, securing flags behind defensive screens of mines and high-ranking soldiers, Rich leaning right over the board as if he was trying to protect his army from aerial bombardment, providing a continuous commentary on moves and strategies, a drone monologue that grated my nerves whenever he and I played L'Attaque together. Some of the pieces were missing, and Rich had made replacements himself, small rectangles cut from out-of-date invitations, the words 'Brigadier' or 'Spy' in his curved, forceful handwriting.

He dwelled on decisions for minutes, thinking aloud, considering the ramifications of each possible move, mindful of exposure and counterattack. I resented these long delays, but Dad was patient, sitting back in his armchair and returning to his book, getting through two or three pages while Rich contemplated the board, brooding on his options.

'I think I've got you!' Dad said, challenging Richard's commander-in-chief.

Rich smiled. He was generous in defeat. 'I thought I'd got *you*,' he said, smiling. 'But you were too good.' He stood alongside Dad and laid his right hand on his left shoulder. 'Too good!'

But then the next day, a black mood descending, Rich lost all capacity for play.

'How about a game of L'Attaque?' Dad said.

'What would I want to do that for?' Rich answered, his forehead creased, a deep, vertical furrow delving between his eyebrows. 'I'm not a baby, you know.'

It was no use saying how much he'd enjoyed it last time: his memory didn't work like that. People with damaged frontal lobes are able to form and retrieve long-term memories, but their recent memory is often affected. For lack of interest, the patient 'forgets to remember'. The frontal patient's inability to plan ahead may be a related deficit: foresight is a kind of 'prospective memory'; the patient lacks the capacity to formulate and carry out plans because he or she has no memory of what is going to happen.

Richard's mood could switch abruptly. Dad had a favourite trick. He broke a piece off his biscuit and placed it carefully on the crown of his scalp.

'Now, don't take your eyes off the biscuit,' he said. He

spread his hand flat over it and started to rub in circles as if he was massaging a bruise. Then he took his hand down and showed us it was empty. There was nothing on his head either, in his silver-white hair, mussed by rubbing. The biscuit had disappeared. He'd rubbed it straight through his head. He opened his mouth and took out the piece of biscuit, holding it up between finger and thumb like a communion wafer.

It didn't matter that I'd known the secret for ages, how he tucked a second piece of biscuit inside his cheek before the whole thing began. Still it was a miracle when that biscuit reappeared, spit-damp, returned to open air after its journey through skull and brain into the mouth.

I'd seen Rich laugh at this along with the rest of us, but when the fury gathers inside him he can't take pleasure in anything.

'It's stupid,' he says, fuming. 'It's for babies. A bunch of babies, that's what you are. There's another piece in his mouth, can't you see? Look.'

He stands over Dad and takes hold of his head, one hand on his jaw, the other across his face, prising his mouth open so he has to reveal the biscuit. Dad doesn't put up any resistance, and after a few seconds Richard relents.

'It's just for stupid babies,' he says again.

Mum and Rich walked up the hill to post some letters. They were on the main road when Rich began to have a seizure. Mum stood between him and the traffic. She felt his weight against her as he lost consciousness and began to fall.

She leaned back against him, his body rigid in the tonic phase, cars passing inches away at high speeds. She couldn't hold him, he was too heavy, but she managed to guide his collapse so he fell along the side of the road rather than straight out into it, convulsions already beginning. She folded her coat to cushion his head and waited.

I came home and left for school again through a period of bludgeoning seizures and aggressive moods, an anger at large inside the moat, explosive, a wildness everyone does their best to appease and keep a distance from. Mum and Dad have asked friends for tea and we're sitting at the almond-shaped table with the two Toby jugs and china figures of highwaymen Tom King and Dick Turpin on horseback in the corner shelves. Rich is upstairs watching television and we all know privately it's better he doesn't come down until the tea party's over and these visitors have gone. But now he appears in the arched doorway, his face swollen with sleep, unshaven, his eyelids heavy.

'Come and join us, Rich,' Dad says, gesturing towards an empty chair. Rich ignores it and instead drags a chair from the far side of the room, setting it in place with a jarring movement, as if the chair were liable to mischief and needed discipline. Nobody said anything. He sat as if it were a means of attack, a sudden release of weight that threatened to crush the chair beneath him, joints and spars protesting.

'How about a cup of tea?' Mum said, looking at him kindly.

'Please,' Rich answered, not looking her.

'Anything good on?' Dad asked.

Rich turned to face him with a sharp glare

'I wouldn't be watching it otherwise.' His frown deep-
ened. 'What a stupid question. I've never heard such a
stupid question.'

He helped himself to sugar, digging the spoon in like
someone shovelling gravel.

Dad returned to the conversation they'd been having
earlier, but Rich wouldn't let go.

'You should think before you speak,' he said, leaning
back, looking down at the table. 'Then maybe you wouldn't
ask such stupid questions.'

Day after day he slept into the afternoon and came
downstairs with swollen eyes, sleep-dazed, deep linen creases
like knife scars across his cheek; for a while, he wouldn't say
anything, or just a few mumbled phrases, as if the power of
speech was waking up more slowly than his other capacities.
But already he was primed for opposition.

Mum warned me to stay out of his way. It had been
raining all week and the moat was close to brimming its
banks: there were flood pools at the bottom of the park and
a lake in Danver's Meadow, sheep crowded on the slope
below the village. Dad was worried about the water level
and wanted to raise the sluice gate so the moat could drain
off into the brook, and when the rain stopped I followed
him across the lawn to the stables shed where Bert kept the
Dennis, logs stacked against the back wall, saws and garden

tools hanging on nails, an iron bar resting in the far corner
– the heavy, rust-covered staff you needed to raise and lower
the sluice.

Carrying the bar over my shoulder I followed Dad
round the moat, past the chestnut pollard and the oak with
Harry Bennett's tree house in it, and past the green mound,
the hillock of dredge-matter I'd visited once a day, reli-
giously. Rooks lifted and circled above us, black on grey, the
iron bar heavy and cold on my shoulder. We ducked under
low yew branches and stood by the sluice gate. Dad fitted
the bar to the ratchet and used all his weight to shift it,
inch by inch, a whirlpool forming as moat water drained
underneath us, the corner scum of leaf mould and duck
slurry breaking up as it slid over the lip of the vortex.

We walked home. I didn't return the bar to the shed but
brought it into the house and left it leaning in the stone
corner of the hall beneath the six-pointed star of black iron
and glass. Richard was in the kitchen.

'Where do you think you've been?' he said.

'We've been lifting the sluice gate,' Dad replied. 'To let
some of the moat out into the brook.'

'What do you want to do that for?'

'Just in case there's more rain. It's almost flooding, you
see.'

Rich was frowning darkly, a fight going on inside him:
he understands the sense of what's been said, but he can't
accept it while another, more dominant self is intent on
conflict.

'What good's that going to do?'

'Well, it might be a safety valve and stop the moat from flooding.'

'Be a what?'

'A safety valve.'

'A safety valve?' He repeated the words with scorn. 'I don't know what you're talking about.'

Dad walked into the kitchen.

'I don't know what you're talking about,' Rich said again.

He followed Dad into the kitchen. I stood in the hall, under the glass star.

'I've never heard anybody talk such a load of trash in all my life.'

Dad didn't say anything. He was at the sink, washing his hands. Richard stood behind him, leaning forward to speak straight into his ear.

'Did you hear me? You talk a load of trash.'

Dad came back out into the hall. Rich followed him. Mum was coming down the spiral staircase.

'A load of trash,' Rich said again. The phrase had worked into his head and found a groove. 'Your husband talks a load of trash.'

'Remember what we talked about,' my mother said. 'About good behaviour, and holidays.'

'Don't you start.' His temper was coiling. 'Don't you start talking that trash. I've had enough of all that trash. Trash, that's all it is. Trash.'

'Come on, Rich,' Dad said, taking his arm.

'Get your hands off me!' Rich shouted, rage spilling over. I backed into the kitchen. I knew we were on the edge of something. I wanted to see what was going to happen. Dad stepped away as Rich wrested his arm free with a violent jerk. The movement swung his whole body round so he faced the stone corner where I'd left the iron bar, and as if he was simply obeying the movement's logic he reached out and picked it up in both hands, then turned to face Mum and Dad at the foot of the stairs, lifting the bar up and back as he took one step and then another towards them.

'Some people here just don't know when to keep their mouths shut,' he said. I looked at his hands gripping the bar and saw that he was shaking. Without warning he swung the bar across in front of him into one of the windows to the left of the stairs, smashed glass falling to the parquet floor. Cold air rushed in as Rich drew the bar back again like a baseball bat and swung it at the second window. I stepped further into the kitchen. My parents were almost at the top of the stairs. For a while Rich didn't move, as if the two explosions had shocked the fury out of him. Then he turned towards me and walked back across the hall. I was ready to run, but he set the bar down again in the same corner I'd left it minutes before. A breeze blew through the glassless windows. Rich drew his right forearm across his nose.

'I've never heard such trash in all my life,' he said.

o

I dreamed the house was under attack. Fighter planes and bombers flew low over the church and stables. The castle thumped and shook with explosions. Bombs fell through the stone slates; the young beech caught fire; jets flew strafing passes over and over. A burning roof timber crashed through the ceiling of Richard's room, flames engulfing the curtains. I ran along corridors, shielding my face against falling stone fragments and bursts of window shrapnel.

I dreamed about floods, the moat brimming its banks, water covering the lawns. I was standing with Bert Dancer in the first-floor room where my parents worked at their desks. We looked down through a trapdoor into flooded stone rooms below us. Outside, water had reached the bottom of the arched window. The rain didn't let up, and we watched as the water crept slowly up the glass. I didn't understand: we were on the first floor – how could the floods possibly rise so high? Then I realized that the floods weren't rising. The house was sinking.

One afternoon I saw Dad standing next to the house, his right arm stretched out, palm pressed flat against a buttress, his head dropped. He didn't move.

'What are you doing?' I asked.

He said he was asking the house for some of its strength.

o

In 1870, at a small hospital for the chronically ill in Pavia, Camillo Golgi began experimenting with a new method of staining nerve cells for examination under the microscope.

Golgi's method, which he called 'the black reaction', only stained a fraction of the cells in each sample. Mounted on a slide and viewed under the microscope, these cells stood out sharply, silver and black on a yellowish background, and Golgi was able to produce detailed drawings of them. In his paper 'On the Structure of the Grey Matter of the Brain', Golgi described the nerve cell body and its 'processes': a single long tubular extension or 'axon' at one end, and several branching extensions or 'dendrites' at the other.

In 1887, the Spanish microanatomist Santiago Ramón y Cajal became Professor of Histology at the University of Barcelona. Using Golgi's silver chromate staining technique, Cajal began to study the structure of the brain. Cajal refined Golgi's method. He examined nerve cells in the embryos of birds and small mammals: these immature cells had yet to develop their fatty coating, and so could be seen with particular definition under the microscope. In 1890 and 1891 alone, Cajal produced twenty-seven books and articles on the fine structure of the nervous system. Where Golgi had shared the widespread belief that nerve cells fused together, forming a continuous net or web, Cajal argued 'that nerve cells should be regarded as independent elements, just like all other cells comprising the body.' The nervous system, Cajal suggested, was made up of individually distinct but connecting nerve cells. He also proposed that signals passed through nerve cells in one direction only: 'The transmission of the nervous impulse is always from the dendritic branches and the cell body to the axon.' Dendrites receive incoming signals from other neurons; axons, which divide into fine branches called collaterals at their tips, carry signals to other neurons. This was Cajal's law of 'dynamic polarization'.

Between October and December 1891, Wilhelm Waldeyer, Director of the Anatomical Institute in the University of Berlin, published six reviews of the latest research into the cell structure of the central nervous system. Waldeyer agreed with Cajal that the terminal extensions – the axons and dendrites – of nerve cells didn't fuse together. Each nerve cell was an independent unit. Waldeyer also proposed a name for these cells that Golgi and Cajal had described so precisely.

He called them neurons.

o

The heron stood by the water. Rooks flew east and west over the house. Joyce sat on her high stool under the wire-gauze domes. Mrs Upton and Mrs Green disappeared into the other end. The moat froze and thawed. Swallows and swifts returned. Mum painted the new flag. Rich carried the saw to Stafford Wood and chose the Christmas tree. The twins came back lit with city glamour. Mr Lewis rang the church bells. Visitors streamed beneath the corbels and gargoyles. My height crept up the measuring wall opposite the laundry room like a high-water mark.

I was happy at school, growing in confidence. When I came home I ran up the stairs to the Barracks and made straight for the secret door. I got my fingers into the gap and prised it open. I waited while my eyes adapted to the dark, heart thumping. In the darkness I could make out the shape of a second door, rimmed with light. I walked towards it. My hands found the bolts and slid them back. I pushed the door open and stepped out into daylight, onto a flat, leaded area among chimneys, enclosed by battlements, rooks cawing overhead, a weathered oak door to my left like the entrance to a stone cottage on top of the house, a hermitage built on the roof. Flakes of rust came off in my hands when I grasped the handle. The door gave a prolonged, waning creak as I pushed it open. I stepped into an empty room: two small, square windows, a fireplace with a cast-iron grate, cobwebs all over, floorboards strewn with plaster fragments and pigeon feathers.

I felt like a trespasser in the Captain of the Guards' Room. When soldiers had slept along the Barracks, the officer in charge had had his own secluded accommodation: now I'd found my way into it without anyone's permission. I stayed close to the door, in case anything moved, my breathing quick and shallow. The room was too ghost-amenable to relax in, the fireplace and row of iron coat-hooks enough to conjure three or four officers sitting round the warmth, sleeves rolled up, their boots in pairs beside the grate. I couldn't stay too long in case I blinked and found the room no longer empty, the Captain of the Guards standing in front of me, no one to hear if I called out. I challenged myself to stand in the room for a count of fifty. I counted out loud, accelerating through the forties.

Then I retraced my steps, running down the stairs, laundry cupboard doors shaking on their latches as I sped past, down again to the Great Hall, sprinting along the Groined Passage, oblivious to corbels, barging through the music-room door to find Joyce pulling on her blue coat, almost one o'clock, an egg pie in the top oven, flagged by tinfoil.

o

I hadn't seen Richard have a tonic-clonic attack for a long time. They came at night, or when he was away at the centre. But I was used to his partial seizures, spells in which his awareness of everything inside and around him seemed temporarily suspended, his eyelids flickering while the rest of us went on eating or talking. I still didn't think of his difference from other people – his mental sluggishness and inflexibility, his irrational and aggressive moods – as a falling-off from some idea of a 'normal' Richard. His otherness was second nature to me.

When film or concert or other marquee crews arrived he lingered all day among the organizers, relishing his intimate connection to the house, fielding their questions – 'How many bedrooms are there? Do you have any ghosts? Where do you put your Christmas tree?' – with solemn concentration, and I noticed his pride in our home, the way his whole person swelled as if it had just woken up to itself and all his vital signs had shifted gear. Visitors deferred to his privileged insight, and Rich seemed enlarged by the realization that he had information and experience others could delight in,

distributing his answers and anecdotes with noble benevolence. They know everything isn't quite right with him, but
they're drawn to his big-spiritedness and enthusiasm, and
soon he's joining them for coffee breaks, showing off his
Leeds United mug like an heirloom tankard, coming to find
Mum in the kitchen to tell her how *extremely* nice Jeff is, or
Andrew, or Elizabeth, then running back to the Great Hall
or Oak Room to lay one hand on his new friends' shoulders,
the Bible weight we were all familiar with.

So Rich was more excited than anyone when prepara-
tions began weeks in advance for a great fair in the park,
volunteers marking out zones with red, white and blue tape,
the grass disappearing acre by acre beneath cars, stalls, beer
tents, straw bales, catering vans, toilets, first-aid points and
administrative Portakabins, megaphone speakers rigged in
the trees.

Mrs Upton and Mrs Green dusted and polished each
nook and surface of the house's public side.

'Many hands make light work,' Mrs Upton said. 'That's
what they say, isn't it? If you've got lots of pairs of hands,
the work doesn't seem so bad, because you've got so many
people doing it.'

'That's right,' Mrs Green agreed. 'You have.'

Bert steered the Dennis like a boat across the lawns. I
went with Dad to fetch floodlights from the stables loft. The
floodlights were tin bowls covered with glass, the filaments
in their fat clear bulbs thick enough for birds to perch on,
and the first talk of them quickened something in me: it was

like the excitement I felt when men opened the backs of film-set trucks and shunted spots and kliegs onto hydraulic platforms, cables in mountaineer coils on their shoulders. Dad only got the floodlights out two or three times a year, and I didn't want to miss it. Rich didn't either. We carried one light each and Rich dashed back for a second, then back again for the heavy transformer block and the yellow cables we had to untangle and lay out in lines converging on the garage door. Dad let Rich angle the lights, and he applied himself with a foreman's seriousness, crouching behind the floodlight and squinting for a bulb's-eye view of the house, tilting the bowl and stepping back to check the angle, each action carried out with slow, other-worldly diligence, as if he were working underwater, as if time were moving through him at a different speed, his inner clock lagging behind our Greenwich mean.

I couldn't wait for the half-dark when Dad said it was OK to turn the floodlights on. He had to lift me so I could flick the switch. The light didn't reach the house immediately: I thought I could see it moving on a broad front, liquid streaming from the bulbs, breaking like a storm-surge against the castle. Stars over the roof disappeared; light gleamed off flaws in the window glass; the four lamps hummed with voltage. I ran in front of them, watching my shadow run across the front of the building. I stepped closer to the lamps, then away from them, looking for the point where my shadow fitted the castle exactly, eaves angled over my forehead like a hat brim, and when I was as tall as my house was I ran back and forth in front of the lights, my shadow sliding across the bays and indentations.

A cloudless day, I followed my sister and two brothers across the bridge into the park, familiar trees poking above vehicles and structures. Police dogs leaped small white show-jump fences and identified criminal suitcases in heaps of decoy bags. Jump-suited bomb-disposal experts ran through emergency routines, a compact remotely-operated machine moving on caterpillar tracks towards suspicious packages. Archers loosed arrows at targets angled like shields; soldiers in felt berets stood round the backs of army trucks dismantling rifles and mortars; a bearded man in green tweed plus-fours swung a baited leash for the hawk perched on his gauntlet cuff. Light sparkled off the moat, the house encircled by a jewelled band, visitors sitting round the edge, jeans rolled up, feet in the water. I knew I had no privileges of admission at the fair, but I felt my familiarity as a kind of ownership: I knew this place better than all the other children; I knew every corner of the house below us, its roof almost white from lack of rain; I knew the park's trees from climbing them or combing the ground beneath them for conkers and acorns. So I walked confidently through the blur of T-shirts, candyfloss, ice-cream cones and sunglasses, through the carnival hubbub of laughter, brass bands and Punch-and-Judy shows, the barrel organs and bagpipe drones, the thick, choral layering of hums and whirrs.

I saw Rich in the crowd. He was standing in front of a

fire tender with a hydraulic ladder on its back, watching a fireman in black and yellow usher people into the operator's cage. The fireman stepped in with them, latched the steel gate shut and pushed a button on a control panel; the tender shook and whirred; the platform began to rise, the passengers like travellers in the basket of a hot-air balloon, waving down at those left behind, then gripping the rim as the cage gained height, the hydraulic booms extending like an arm from shoulder and elbow until the cage of people resembled Liberty's torch, held aloft in the blue.

I forgot about the rest of the fair. I kept looking at the fireman's cage, rising above the fray. Richard wanted to go up in it. He told me to wait in the queue while he found Mum and Dad. He didn't take long. We watched families ahead of us ascend into the sky. Minutes before, they'd been undistinguished, part of the crowd; now they were the elect, looking down at us, as if they were our representatives, going up into that extensive bird region on our behalf, to bring back news. They gripped the waist-height rail as the cage shuddered and began to rise. They took one hand off the rail and waved at us. We kept our eyes on the cage as it rose higher and higher; we already saw ourselves in it.

I could feel heat coming off the tender, sun glaring off polished steel fenders and valves.

'Are you sure you want to go up?' Dad said. 'You won't be able to get off once we're on.'

'I want to go,' I said.

'How about you, Rich?'

'Nothing's going to stop me going.'

The hydraulic arm was at full extension now, high over-head. For a while, they stayed up there, the booms locked straight. Then the truck shuddered again; the arm retracted, bending at the base and midway joints; the cage settled on top of the tender. The family group was laughing, exhila-rated, shaking hands with the operator; they helped each other down off the red engine in a show of attentiveness and fellow-feeling.

'Good luck!' they said, as they passed us, merging into the crowd.

I went first, climbing up onto the tender.

'OK, then,' the fireman said. 'In you go, that's right.'

He latched the steel gate shut and told us to hold on. He said that if we felt queasy or scared we should just let him know, he'd take us down straightaway. He said it was perfectly safe, the boom could support a much greater weight than us.

'I'm not so sure about that,' Rich said, patting his tummy, smiling.

The fireman pushed a button. The platform shook; the rail vibrated against my hands; I waved at our neighbours in the queue as we started our ascent, their faces shrinking. We climbed smoothly, without jerk or surge, and soon we were eye-level with rooks, above the seethe and bustle of the fair: balloons and hats crowding the lanes; St John's Ambulance volunteers on deckchairs outside the first-aid station; Morris dancers in the arena marked out by straw bales; a steam engine moving like a dinosaur among the tents and caravans. It was a surprise, how quickly the noise receded: children shouting, carousel music, the shimmer of accordions and tambourines. We looked down at the house, the sere green lawns and water-sparkle, and out over fields, woods and farm buildings, as if we were surveying the area on a map, picking out features: Frederick's Wood, Stafford Wood, Thomas's Plantation and Miller's Osiers, Madmarston Hill and Jester's Hill, the Sor Brook lined with silver-leaved cricket-bat willows, chicken sheds in the yard at Fulling Mill, trees above the ruined village called Hazelford. The town's outskirts encroached over the hills. Juno's white head gleamed.

The arm was at full extension.

'This is it,' the fireman said. 'This is as far as we go, I'm afraid.'

It was far enough. I could see for miles. The world curved beneath us. Richard had both hands on the rail as if he were standing on the top deck of a ship, a liner leaving port for open sea.

THREE

I CAME HOME from school to find Mrs Upton, Mrs Green, Mrs Dancer and Harry Bennett sitting round the kitchen table, the white glass sphere suspended above them in the medieval vaults, Joyce on her high perch beneath the fly-guards, Bert Dancer arriving with yew needles caught in his sleeveless V-neck sweater.

'What time do you call this?' Mrs Dancer asked, looking at her watch, teasing.

Joyce made me a hot chocolate just like Bert's and I sat at the green table, eating biscuits.

'What was the house like?' I asked. 'In the war?'

I was thinking of the Great Hall stacked with specimens from the Natural History Museum, animals coming alive at night and forcing the lids.

'Full of evacuees,' Harry began. 'On account of there was all the bombing. There were these two old ladies living here, Mrs Kimber and her sister. One of them was blind. And there was this young fellow – he's dead now. Came here as a young gardener and slept in the Captain of the Guards' Room, up on the leads. And he stepped out of there one night and found himself face to face with Mrs Kimber, and she was carrying a candle – she always had a candle so some-body could see her – and he saw this white person and bolted out the castle, and he never came back. They never saw him again.'

'Mrs Kimber,' Joyce said. 'I used to take her breakfast up.'

'Then there was that other time,' Mrs Upton said. 'At the almshouses.'

'The almshouses, that's right,' Harry said. He swallowed the skin off the top of his coffee. Everyone looked at him, waiting.

'This was one evening I went down to see old Eli Hirons,' he began. 'He wanted me to decorate his kitchen up. I sat there chattering and had a very good supper, because his wife was a wonderful cook, and this was forced on me, more or less. After that I got my bicycle and walked up the hill and then I see this as I got to the top, you know, by the almshouses.'

'Go on then,' Mrs Dancer encouraged him.

'The first thing I saw was this little old lady, grey-haired. It was towards the end of the war, and it was double summertime while the war was on – it must have been quarter to eleven at night and you could still see then, at that time. And this old lady came down that wall, creeping down the wall. She was in a bustle and a blouse, like they used to wear, and she stopped immediately opposite the almshouse gate and went in. So of course I thought, "Well, that's amusing, that is," and I had a good mind to see where she's gone. Then just when I was thinking of that, this appearance of this vicar stood there, looking across into the almshouses, and he was a tall, thin chap, I should put him at about fifty, and he's got his black cassock, how they used to wear them, and a belt around him. And I thought, I don't know, "This is getting interesting!" So I gently walked round the road and in the top cottage was a lady, a district nurse named Stopford, lived with her old father. And he appeared there the next, the vicar, looking across to our window. Of course I didn't know what to do, whether to go up and try to speak to him or not. So anyway I dived up my steps, hid my bike in the privet hedge and sat waiting for him to come down to look into our house. Well, I sat there for at least a quarter of an hour and never see him again; there was nobody at all when I went down those steps. He'd completely vanished. And they were as plain as if it were me and you looking at one another.'

He paused. Nobody said anything while he ate the rest of his biscuit.

'When was this, Harry?' Mrs Green asked.

'August.'

'No, I mean what year was it?'

'1944, it must have been.'

Harry drank some more of his coffee.

'Anyway,' he said. 'When I went to work next morning, there's this fellow worked with me named Fletcher, and I told him about it. "Oh," he said, "I know who you're talking about. My old Gramp told me about that years ago

– it's the almshouse ghost that you've seen." The almshouse ghost! So I never see him again, this vicar, and I was rather disappointed because I thought afterwards, I wish I'd have went off and spoke and seen what reaction I got.'

'You probably scared him off,' Mrs Dancer said. 'Gave him a fright, you hiding in that hedge, I should imagine.'

'I should think I did,' Harry said, laughing.

o

Richard had been getting into trouble at the centre. He kept having arguments. He'd punched members of staff and fellow residents; he'd headbutted a nurse, a woman. He was twenty-five. He wasn't allowed home for Easter after persistent bad behaviour.

'All the more good for me, as I wouldn't have known, otherwise,' he told Mum on the telephone, full of remorse.

At home, he moved between bed and the TV, coming downstairs with a deep-scored frown, intent on conflict, black eyebrows angled together. He threw our food into the bin and made his own, fry-ups smoking out the ground floor, hunks of meat and cheese wedged onto the plate. He couldn't stop himself eating cheese, so Mum started hiding it: blocks of Cheddar in chests-of-drawers, half-Stiltons among lanterns and candles. The burglar alarm went off past midnight and I followed Dad downstairs to the Groined Passage and Great Hall, expecting burglars. We saw a figure moving under the suits of armour and Dad swung the torch-beam onto it.

'Switch that bloody thing off,' Rich said, squinting at the glare. He'd gone into the other end to search cupboards for cheese.

If he comes to meals at all he shows up late; the joints protest as he tips back on the chair; he flicks the salt and pepper shakers like Subbuteo players, sending them skidding along the grain; he picks up a knife and bangs the handle hard on the table repeatedly, a remorseless beat such as oarsmen had to keep time to in triremes.

'Please don't do that, Rich,' Dad says. 'It's not very peaceful for the rest of us.'

'Who asked for your opinion?' he grunts back. 'You better shut your face. You better keep your mouth shut.'

'There's no need for that.'

'I don't know what you're talking about.'

Rich tipped back on his chair again.

'Some people here talk far too much,' he went on, addressing empty air above the table. 'Some people here need to watch their mouths.'

We eat in silence while Rich helps himself from dishes on the stove. Mum and Dad urge him to be moderate – 'Now remember what we said, about moderation' – but he heaps food into a mound like a molehill, thumps the plate down and drags the chair under him so it scrapes on the linoleum. The violence in his gestures seems deliberately deployed to shake us from an apathy we're not even aware of, to provoke us to intensities of feeling equal to the rage his body's a barely adequate vessel for. Suddenly he stops eating and freezes as if in a game of musical statues, the knife and fork halfway from plate to mouth; his stare holds blankly on an in-between distance and his eyelids flutter, the corner of his mouth twitching. It's as if the personality we know as 'Richard' has disappeared, as if his selfhood has vanished, as if time is flowing past but not through him, the way a river flows round a boulder, and nobody says anything while it's going on. I'm sitting opposite Richard and I watch him closely, confused, because he seems to be here and not here at the same time, and as the seizure passes Mum reaches out to lay her hand on his upper arm in reassurance, his aggression already forgotten.

Sometimes I went with my parents when they drove Richard to the station. We'd stop outside the tobacconist's on East Bar and wait while Rich stocked up on tobacco and lighter fuel, and then wait on the platform as the train pulled in and Rich picked up the Leeds United holdall none of the rest of us could manage single-handed. His dark mood hadn't entirely lifted, but now it was mixed with shame, regret over the way he'd behaved, his tenderness restored, as if the imminence of departure had forced a shift of perspective. He knew which end of the platform to stand for the smoking carriage, and we watched through the window as he heaved the stuffed blue and gold bag onto the overhead rack and pushed it in as far as it would go, then pushed again with both hands until it was jammed. He sat down next to the window and smiled, embarrassed by the attention; he pretended to ignore us, reaching into his plastic bag for his pipe and *Daily Mirror*, before he couldn't restrain himself any longer and broke into a grin, waving as the train first jolted then rolled north towards Leamington and Coventry.

o

I was fourteen. I was still sleeping in the dressing room, next to my parents. I hadn't wanted to sleep alone on the second floor, out of earshot. I hadn't wanted to risk the dark in rooms adjoining the other end, only a door between me and the eerie uninhabited spaces of the Kings' Chamber, Great Parlour, Long Gallery and Barracks. But my teenager's desire for independence got the better of my fear, and I moved upstairs to a room off the Gallery, with Martin's old stereo and a plunder of his tapes and records. I took my adolescent grumpiness up here and didn't bother to turn the volume down when I heard tour groups moving along the Gallery the other side of the white door, the guides' descriptions of seventeenth-century glazing and plasterwork soundtracked by drums and electric guitars.

The twins shared city flats with friends. They came home with talk of boyfriends, girlfriends, music, London. I was in awe of their worldliness and hungry for it but shy to ask too many questions, reluctant to flag my ignorance or draw attention to the moat limit I lived within. Rich was older still but inhabited a limbo medium all his own, child and adult at the same time, his days divided between our moated castle and his cubicle bedroom at the epilepsy centre.

I started to look for ways of being alone, self-reliant, away from Richard and my parents. I wanted, even within the circle of the moat, to be beyond observation. So I disappeared into the Barracks or out onto the castle's roofs, scrambling across leads and stone slates, settling in secret enclosures like pockets among dunes, rooks crossing overhead between the worm-rich park and their rendezvous trees.

I'd only really known the square of flat roof at the east end, accessed by a door from the laundry room, eye-level with rooks' nests in lime and chestnut crowns across the water, two lengths of old electrical flex strung as washing-lines between the house and battlements. Every two or three yards the roofing leads overlapped in thin ridges, and these raised seams were perfect for tightrope-walking while Mum pegged damp clothes out on lines too high for me to reach, drips from towel or sheet corners leaving dark archipelago splotches on the grey-white leads. I'd helped my parents lug two old mattresses out here, and we'd slept under a sky crisscrossed by washing-lines, so much sun-heat in the leads it was like having an electric blanket switched on beneath you; I'd woken to Dad's sonorous two-part snores in the dark and a salt-grain abundance of stars, battlements inked in like a code of presence and absence, a first-light downpour driving us inside before the rooks got started.

But now that washing-line roof space was too easy to get to, too much an extension of our domestic realm, too low for any summit euphoria or sensation of escape. Better to

climb three storeys up the west stairs and go out through
the low-cut timber door beyond the Council Chamber –
no battlements here, just a wall with bevelled topstones
visitors would rest their hands or forearms on, leaning over
vertiginous drops, gazing across the box fleurs-de-lys and
circles of the Ladies' Garden, the open lawns, the river-
broad moat, the water meadows and sloping park beyond
it, as if they were travellers pausing on the brink of a high
escarpment, unknown country spread out below.

I liked this roof's balcony prominence, the cliff-edge
feeling of exposure and altitude, and I spent hours lying on
the few yards of open leads between the wall and the slope
of tiles, watching clouds and rooks pass over, daydreaming
about girls. One section of lead was covered with graffiti:
rudimentary outlines of hands and shoes cut into the metal,
names and dates inscribed with ornate, antiquated slants:
W Lambert 1815; IMS 1795; J Bradfield 1885. I tried the
fit of my hands and feet inside the outlines; I noticed when
visitors added their signatures to the panel; I got angry
whenever a new name appeared, as if something private
and sacred had been encroached upon and spoiled – as
if someone had tattooed their name on my forearm while
I slept: I wanted to gouge it out.

Harry Bennett was at home on the roofs.

'I remember one evening I was coming home and there
was this terrific glow on the roof,' he said in the kitchen.
'It was lighting up the sky. So I went and banged on Bert's
door and got on the phone and got hold of the fire brigade.

I thought, I better dash down there and find out whatever's the matter, and when I got in I went straight up onto the roof and I'll be damned if the chimney wasn't on fire! The fire brigade came and I shouted down to them where I was and how to get up there. Of course they just swilled the place with water and put it out, it was a good mess. What had happened was, there was a jackdaw's nest in part of it and that had caught fire and set the whole chimney ablaze. And all the other chimneys, every one when I first came here was completely blocked with jackdaw nests. I had a job getting up to all those chimneys and clearing them of jackdaw nests, putting wire over some of them too.'

I'd seen Harry working on the roof, tying one end of a rope round his paunch, looping the rest round a chimney and securing it with amateurish granny knots. Safety system in place, he climbed a ladder laid against the tiles, then moved onto the tiles themselves, flattening himself starfish-like against the slope, inching toward a small, distant gap where thin white laths showed through, the rope slack below him, and then he got his hammer out and banged fresh nails in like a mountaineer fixing pitons.

One afternoon, confident no one was looking, I embarked on this final ascent myself, aiming for the chimney summits, spreading my weight across the tiles as I'd seen Harry spread his, stone slates shifting and clattering beneath me. I got about a third of the way when a tile cracked under my knee and a fragment skidded loose, exposing the top of the tile underneath to open air for the first time in more than four hundred years. It stood out with sad, unhealthy pallor, unweathered, and I looked at the sudden bareness with a stab of remorse, not because I feared reprimand or punishment but because of some idea I had that the house was a sentient being, vulnerable to injury. I slid back to the leads and brushed the moss and lichen off my shirt, closing the roof door behind me with special care as if by attention I could make good the damage.

o

After repeated warnings, Richard was expelled from the epilepsy centre. Nowhere else would take him, given his record of violent behaviour. Now, whenever I came home from school, my brother was already there, his lethargy and lack of motivation worse than ever. He slept into the afternoon, then watched TV into the night, falling asleep in front of it. He didn't wash or shave. He communicated through the same limited set of threatening expressions: 'Mind your own business'; 'You should keep your mouth shut'; 'I don't have to; you can't make me.'

He was having one or two general tonic-clonic fits every month, as well as several partial seizures. Sometimes, coming round in the aftermath, he described the aura, the sensations before he lost consciousness: he talked about 'a fizziness', 'a clinging on one side'; he said he'd felt as if he'd had ice in his tummy, as if 'the ground was all sliding on the top'.

'Everything's there that wasn't there,' he said, coming

round from a severe tonic-clonic seizure. 'It's just like being in another world.'

He didn't remember arriving at the hospital in Oxford.

'How did I get here?' he asked. He had a vague memory of car lights. 'I'm dreaming and then I wake up and I do what I'm dreaming.'

'R fell – foam but no shaking, or hardly any,' Mum wrote in her notebook after another attack. 'Not hearing us, lay there for ten minutes. Got into car. Said, "Aren't we going the wrong way, in not out?" Sat and smoked. I told him what had happened. About 20 mins after attack, I told him again what had happened and he said, "Did I? Did I come back in the car? Did I smoke?" He didn't remember any of that.'

After one tonic-clonic seizure he sat in a chair, gripping the armrests.

'I'm shaking to pieces,' he said. 'Things have been so horrible for me.'

Still, most of the seizures came at night. Mum found him sitting on the edge of his bed in his pyjamas, confused, his eyelids flickering, the bed wet with urine. She washed him and took him downstairs; later, he had no recollection of being washed, no idea how he'd got downstairs.

He's subdued in the days afterwards, without energy, the wind knocked out of him. Slowly his strength returns. He rides the racing bike full-tilt along the drive and wallops tennis balls against the wall beside the kitchen window, bits of house flaking off at each impact. He watches golf and snooker tournaments from start to finish, sitting close to the TV, elbows on his knees, leaning forward so the chair balances on its front legs. There are sunlit heron days when Rich helps Mum and Dad with castle jobs, or smokes his pipe in the Ladies' Garden, or wears his suit and a bow tie for a concert in the church, his hand on Mum's shoulder to engage her attention as he reports a pun:

'If somebody wanted a bodyguard *and* a gardener, couldn't they just have a *bodyguardner*?'

He came in through the back door into the hall, hands clasped together and held out in front of him as if he'd just trapped a butterfly in them.

'Where's Dad?' he asked.

'I don't know,' I said. 'What is it?'

'It's a baby swift. We've got to call the vet.' He opened his hands the way you'd imitate a book opening, and I saw the young swift lying motionless on his palm, wings flat against its body. I'd never seen a swift this close. It was tiny, grey; its eyes were shut; it lay dead still. Rich was worked up, pacing back and forth, his brain racing.

'Where's Mum?' he asked.

'I don't know.'

'Are you sure you haven't seen Dad?'

'Yes.'

'I'm going to call the vet.' He went over to the telephone, then paused: he didn't know how to pick up the receiver and dial while he still held the baby swift in his hands.

'Will you call the vet?' he asked. 'Tell them it's urgent. It's *very* important.'

But the next day his mood had changed, the thunder-cloud expression in his face, every moment an occasion for conflict.

'Get out of my way,' Rich said. We were passing each other on the spiral stairs. 'Don't you look where you're going?'

'You might have given me some room,' I answered.

'What's that?'

'I said you might have given me some room.'

'You should look where you're going. You should think about looking where you're going.'

He was one step up, glaring down at me.

'You only had to give me some room,' I repeated.

'I didn't ask for your opinion. You should try keeping your mouth shut.'

'I'm only saying—'

'Didn't you hear me? Didn't I tell you to keep your mouth shut?'

'I don't care. You should have given me some room.'

'I told you to keep your mouth *shut*,' he said, raising his fist. 'Do you want this in the face? Someone's going to get this in the face, if they're not careful.'

I'd seen and heard enough to know Rich could act on his threats. But I felt immune; I was sure he wouldn't hurt me. Perhaps I imagined my mother and father would step between us, or that in Richard's eyes I would always be the infant arriving home from the maternity ward, eleven years younger, beyond violence. Still, I'm aware of how much bigger than the rest of us he is – fourteen stone, with a bear's strength in his arms, his footsteps upstairs on the loose carpeted boards a specific thunder you could follow from rooms away. We entrusted jam jars with impossible lids to him (holding the jar in his left hand he'd clamp his right on top and quickly force the seal) and when the boat or punt filled with rainwater overnight we needed Richard with us to heave the craft onto its side and ready it for launching. But his violent language recasts his bulk and strength as resources of harm and I know I'm not a match for them.

'Some people round here are asking for trouble,' he said.

o

The neurologist John Hughlings Jackson moved from York to London in 1862 to begin work at the National Hospital for the Relief and Cure of the Paralysed and Epileptic. Wishing to escape 'the great vagueness of the word "epilepsy"', Jackson wrote detailed descriptions of hundreds of his patients' seizures: jerks and twitches, dreamy states, sensory hallucinations, the momentary inability to move a limb or understand words. When he dissected the brains of epileptic patients who'd died while in his care, Jackson often found visibly damaged tissue. This brain damage had many causes – head injuries, tumours, temporary loss of oxygen or blood – but the lesions always correlated with seizure states.

Jackson theorized that damaged cells in or around a

lesion sometimes produce 'discharges', and that whenever this happens, a seizure occurs. 'A convulsion,' he proposed in 1870, 'is but a symptom, and implies only that there is an occasional, an excessive, and a disorderly discharge of nerve tissue on muscles. This discharge occurs in all degrees; it occurs with all sorts of conditions of ill health, at all ages, and under innumerable circumstances.' The manifestation and severity of a seizure, Jackson suggested, depends on where in the brain the discharge happens, and how widely it spreads. He distinguished 'generalized' seizures (in which he imagined the discharge spreading rapidly across the brain, causing the person to lose consciousness, fall down and convulse) from 'focal' or 'localized' seizures in which the discharge was confined to a limited region of the brain.

Epilepsy, Jackson concluded in 1873, was 'the name for occasional, sudden, excessive, rapid and local discharges of grey matter.' According to this definition, there wasn't just one disease, epilepsy, but many epilepsies. 'Even a sneeze', Jackson wrote, 'is a sort of healthy epilepsy.'

At first, Jackson didn't know the nature of these disturbances. Then Fritsch, Hitzig and Ferrier showed that the application of electric currents to a small region of the cortex could irritate local groups of muscles, and that stronger currents could lead to convulsions; Bartholow's electrodes induced a seizure in Mary Rafferty; Richard Caton recorded electrical signals in the brains of animals. These results reinforced Jackson's belief that localized convulsions indicated localized injuries to the brain, and that convulsions spread across more of the body as the discharges spread through more of the brain. And they suggested that the 'nerve force' involved in these discharges was electricity.

The brain contains approximately a hundred billion neurons, each communicating with thousands of others through its axon and dendrites. Neurons are surrounded by a much greater number of support cells called glial cells. Charged particles – especially potassium, sodium, calcium and chloride ions – pass in and out of neurons through channels in the cell membrane. This exchange of ions generates an electrical impulse known as an action potential. The impulse travels along the neuron's axon and its collaterals to junctions formed with the dendrites of other neurons. At these junctions, or synapses, the action potential triggers the release of a chemical neurotransmitter, which may prompt the next neuron to 'fire' in turn. These electrical and chemical processes carry information through the nervous system. An axon can convey electrical signals along distances up to three metres, at speeds up to a hundred metres per second.

Such tiny electrical impulses are constantly being produced in the brain. Usually, this electrical discharge is coordinated. But during a seizure, a random, unregulated electrical discharge spreads through the brain. Repetitive inappropriate firing of one neuron might trigger adjacent neurons, so that more and more neurons are incorporated into an abnormal pattern of activity. As Jackson suggested, these paroxysmal discharges manifest themselves in different ways, according to which part of the brain they're happening in and how long they last. If the seizure happens in the motor cortex, the initial manifestation will be a contraction of muscles in the opposite side of the body. If the discharging neurons are in the temporal lobes, the paroxysmal discharge may result in hallucinations, dreamy states or distortions of memory. If the seizure discharge spreads through large areas of the brain, then consciousness may be lost.

o

Spiders roamed the iron rivets and pale oak timbers of the outer door. Here's Harry Bennett to fix a leaking tap, in blue overalls and black boots with rigid steel hutches inside to guard the toes; here's Geoffrey Riley at teatime on Friday to discuss the health of the estate, manila folders under his arm; here's Mrs Green leaning her bicycle on the Chapel buttress; here's John Taylor with a tray of eggs from Fulling Mill; here's Joyce wiping her feet on the bristled door mat; here are the longbowmen to loose a flight of honour from the gatehouse roof; here's the secretary of the Yorkshire Dales Caravan Club to tell my parents the knobbly-knee competition is starting at five o'clock and would they be the judges?

Here's Mr Moulder to report on beech saplings in Frederick's Wood, stooping so he doesn't bash his forehead on the arch.

He walked into the kitchen with slow, deliberate care, as

if all around were fine vases he was frightened of knocking over.

'How are them woods getting on, Mr Moulder?'

'Not too bad, thanks, Joyce.'

He was the tallest man I knew, a totem pole in faded blue boilersuit and enormous mud-caked boots, with a soft voice, and squiggles of blue veins in ruddy countryman's cheeks. For years I'd watched Dad and Mr Moulder set off through the gatehouse arch to check new beech trees in Frederick's or Stafford Wood, or Norway spruce in Thomas's Plantation, or plant a line of oaks at the top of the Bretch, Dad in his green wellingtons and darker green waxed jacket and tweed cap walking briskly to keep up with Mr Moulder's giant blue stride, tilting his head almost to the shoulder to look at Mr Moulder's face when he was speaking.

After Dad stepped in a rabbit hole and sprained his ankle, Mr Moulder carried him home. I was in the kitchen with my mother and we both looked up as the two men came through the gatehouse towards us, Mr Moulder carrying my father in his arms like a bride.

They'd planted a horse chestnut where the single-track road forked beyond the Great Ground. The tree was fifteen years old when people came in the night and cut its branches off. We were walking to Hazelford when we noticed the bare trunk, a long spike footed in a heap of branches. Dad pressed one hand against the tree, as if he were feeling for its pulse, and shook his head, wondering aloud why anyone would do such a thing. They'd sawn flush to the trunk, leaving a tall rod tapering to a point, pale welts up and down it where the branches had joined.

'It's worse than if they'd just chopped it down,' Dad said.

I assumed the tree was dead. But the next spring, it put out shoots. Short twigs pushed through woundwood; sticky, treacle-brown buds opened into leaf; the twigs thickened into branches; the branches formed a crown. Year by year, the chestnut recovered its outline and vigour. Each time I walked past it I remembered the shorn trunk and heap of limbs. Then one afternoon, walking alone, I found the blackened wreck of a burned-out car abandoned against the chestnut. The wreck was still smoking; the fire had scorched off half the tree; there was a long, charred gash in the trunk. But even that didn't finish it off. Woundwood crept over the gulch. New shoots pushed out in the spring.

Mum and Dad had planted the beech in front of the stables not long after I was born. The old copper beech leaned over the moat, roots protruding from the earth in ridges like the bones in the back of an old man's hand. A hawthorn grew out horizontally from a bank halfway up the park, a seaside tree threshed by gales, its trunk a gnarled cord of sinews twisted together, driftwood-smooth where sheep had rubbed their backs and haunches on it, wool tufts snagged on the bark, a scoop of bare ground underneath where hoof friction had seen off the grass. The veteran ash at the bottom of the field called the Shoulder of Mutton, close to the Sor Brook, was two or three hundred years old, short and squat, covered in burrs, with bulbous growths round the base, its main branches long since gone. This ash was hollow, heartwood rotten, and you could crawl into it and look up at a disc of sky as if you were looking up a ship's funnel: I used my hands and feet to wedge myself in and inch towards the light.

Sometimes I went with Dad and Mr Moulder to look at trees, falling behind as they strode across fields, discussing proportions of blackthorn, hawthorn and hazel in hedges, or the best spots for planting new clumps or lines. I carried whips (infant trees, smaller than saplings, root-clods swinging like pendulum weights) and learned to recognize the smooth pale grey bark and black buds of ash trees, the slender pointed buds of beech, the fat treacle buds of horse chestnuts and the leaves and habits of sycamores, field maples, cherries and limes, even as I felt the strengthening of some inner resistance to my father's knowledge and enthusiasms, because I was fifteen, hungry for my own interests and attachments. I wanted to see my friends; I wanted to take the train to the city; I wanted to go to parties. I didn't want to go on holiday with my parents any more, those weeks on canal boats, trips in the camper van to the Black Mountains, along Hadrian's Wall, around the D-Day beaches in Normandy. At home I felt myself turning inward and sullen, bored of fishing, bicycling, rowing the boat, tired of our moated world. I sat in my room for hours, listening to records, dreaming.

'He's a bit back-sunned, that field,' Mr Moulder said, pointing.

I heard their tree talk on the outskirts of my attention.

'Those beech are doing well in Frederick's, where we put the nurse crop in, those softwoods with them.'

You had to stretch your sense of time and imagine how a tree would appear from different viewpoints in fifty or a hundred or even two hundred years.

'This looks like a good spot,' Dad said. 'What do you think?'

I didn't answer. I just dug the hole, standing with both feet on the spade's shoulders to force it down. Mr Moulder held the whip by the neck and lowered the root-plate into the earth; I side-footed the soil back in around it. We checked the progress of saplings in plastic wraparound guards, pruning off lower shoots to encourage each tree to grow straight, to concentrate its energies upwards.

Dad and Mr Moulder admired the splash of skyline trees like the Turkey oaks along the top of the Great Ground. Together they planted oaks in the park, and along hedges and ridges across the estate, and in December they planted cricket-bat willows along the Sor Brook and in the marshy area between Hazelford and Millers' Osiers. This damp ground was perfect for cricket-bat willows. You didn't need to dig, you just sunk a hole with an iron planting bar and pushed the set straight in, a long, bare stick without roots or leaves, a post alongside, a plastic spiral guard to protect the bark from rabbits and deer. The sets went in alternately, one side of the stream and then the other, and twice a year we'd go and see them, rubbing or pruning off shoots below the crown in May: branches meant knots in the grain, and knots were useless in cricket bats. After he'd checked a willow Dad had a way of sweeping his hand up and down the trunk and then patting it quickly before we moved on, as if it were a horse he'd just been grooming. I carried the secateurs and pruning saw, waiting to deal with thicker branches, to join in with the man's work and demonstrate my competence.

Dad wanted to inspect the oaks he and Mr Moulder had planted along one edge of the Great Ground. I waited while he set one foot and then the other on the buttress ledge and leaned over to lace his boots.

'Are we off?' he asked.

'We're off.'

I followed him diagonally across the front lawn towards the gatehouse. I stopped on the bridge, leaning over the wall to check for pike. Confetti pieces were trodden into the metalled drive outside the church gate, paper hearts and horseshoes. We walked across the park and climbed the stile in the top corner, continuing down the lane along the bottom of the Great Ground. The field had just been ploughed: it looked as if someone had dragged a comb through the reddish earth, ridges and furrows accentuating the curve, the line that dipped and rose to the ridge where mature Turkey oaks stood against the blue.

I kept my eye on the Great Ground as we walked, a patch of scrubby woodland on our left, black plastic refuse sacks dumped along the edge, cans and wrappers spilling out where the sacks had snagged open on barbed wire.

'Oh,' Dad said.

He was looking into the wood; I stood level with him and followed his gaze to the car. A white saloon had pulled off the lane and driven in among the trees through a gap in the fence. You couldn't tell if anyone was inside: the window was tinted near-black. I knew Dad was worried someone had dumped it. He looked up and down the lane, but it was just the two of us, the wide open swell of the Great Ground at our backs, the scrubby wood with the strange white car in front. Dad walked towards it. He made for the left side; I veered off to the right; we reached the back doors at the same time. The side windows were tinted too, but not so dark I couldn't see in. A man was sitting in the middle of the back seat. A woman was sitting on his lap, facing him, moving on his lap, her skirt hitched right up above her hips. I stepped away. I hoped they hadn't seen me. Dad was already walking back towards the lane, towards the Great Ground. I followed him. We pushed through a gap in the hedge and strode into the openness of the field.

o

A year passed before my parents found a place for Richard at another centre. Preliminary assessment reported frontal-lobe damage, mainly in the left hemisphere, as well as temporal-lobe impairment, caused or exacerbated by a history of head injuries. The psychologists talked about his diminished executive function, his inability to exercise self-control over his emotional or anger responses. They said his behaviour was especially difficult to manage because his IQ was close to normal: Richard perceived himself as a competent adult; others expected him to understand implications and conse-quences and to behave accordingly; he gave the impression he was more able than he really was. 'He's both fit and unfit,' Mum wrote. 'He's not in a category.'

New drugs reduced his seizures to an average of one tonic-clonic attack every two months. My parents wrote letters and notes to Richard telling him how important it was not to be rude or aggressive; they tried to make a con-nection between his good behaviour and the frequency of his visits home. But hardly a day passed without at least one violent or aggressive outburst, often physical. The police were called when Richard attacked a member of staff. Then a fellow resident attacked him: the cut in his head needed stitches. Another incident led to the police being called again, and Richard received his second official caution.

'Problems this last weekend, I'm afraid,' my mother wrote. 'The pattern has been the same on his last three visits – much that was excellent and easy, but then a sudden thundercloud expression, and a rage in him that is truly frightening, both to us and to him. Afterwards he was distraught, crying and regretting all he had said, and hating himself for the impossibility of control. He did seem to understand that this show of temper is impossible for us, and we equally feel sure that it is way beyond him to control once it has taken root. Almost the worst thing is the distress of Richard himself at the havoc he causes.'

A letter arrived from the centre. 'I have to inform you that there was an incident last night involving Richard and another client, and Richard sustained a laceration above his eye and a laceration to his head. Five stitches had to be inserted.' By now his face was a ledger of injuries: a scar on his nose where a fit felled him on the angle of a friend's doorstep; another on his left ear where a fellow resident clocked him full swing with a cereal bowl; a false front tooth that was smoother and whiter than all the rest, the old one knocked out in a soccer-related brawl. For a while Rich took it out before meals, the wet tooth glistening on our kitchen table like a pearl. I saw a copy of his daily report sheet for one week in June: 'Richard was asked by staff not to eat in TV room. Richard kept asking where the rule was to stop him eating in TV room. Came into office, headbutted staff, ripped a letter on desk into little pieces then went back and watched TV.' When one of the staff asked him not to take a sandwich into the lounge, Richard punched him in the face, and when another member of staff intervened Richard started shouting at him, pushing and kicking. The report described his mood, day by day: 'Aggressive'; 'Very aggressive'; 'Very unsettled'; 'Just waiting to have a go at someone.'

His drug list was longer than ever: lamotrigine, carbamazepine, risperidone, diazepam, clobazam, lorazepam, haloperidol, procyclidine, chlorpromazine, sertraline. A psychologist's report listed his 'problem behaviours': great difficulty with motivation; severe problems with impulse control, leading at times to aggressive behaviour; lack of personal hygiene; difficulty in getting started; difficulty, once started, in stopping; inability to plan and sequence behaviour; disinhibition; unable to problem-solve; insensitive to social cues; inability to learn from feedback; perseveration; tunnel vision; rigidity. 'He cannot take into account the effect of his behaviour on others,' the report noted, 'nor can he always exercise sufficient self-control to behave appropriately.'

'R does not have brakes,' Mum scribbled in the margin.

'Day Services have reported that they believe Richard cannot help his behaviour problems as they are illness-related rather than person-related,' the report continued. And this was a way of saying that it wasn't Richard but his illness that was being 'verbally and physically aggressive', that his behaviour wasn't the same thing as his nature, that Richard wasn't responsible for his words and actions, that free will wasn't granted to him as it was to others. The behavioural traits that antagonized people around him were characteristic of frontal-lobe impairment, but they seemed intended by him, as if he'd considered all the options and chosen belligerence and confrontation. With Richard you had somehow to suspend your instinct to hold people accountable for their behaviour, and understand that what seemed bloody-minded or aggressive was not actually the individual's fault: it wasn't person-related. 'One should not consider the notion that Richard himself can change,' the psychologist noted.

Mum tore a page from her notebook and wrote MEMO TO RICHARD along the top. 'A list of things you might do – or that we might help to arrange – to make your life better. I want to make your life better.' She suggested table tennis, games like L'Attaque, music and singing. But then more news arrived from the centre. Richard had had another fight, this time with a female resident.

'She'd been getting at me,' he explained. 'Accusing me of doing things. We don't get on well. She's the only one I don't get on with. She was giving me orders, saying they were house rules, though I knew jolly well they weren't. Or if they were, there was nothing written down about it.'

He was ashamed of himself, full of regret.

'I knew that spell was going to come to an end some-time,' he said. 'I could see it wasn't going to go on forever. I have never been so worried as I was today. Things have been going so well until then. They've been altering my pills a little. If only they'd left my pills.'

I saw the Notice of Bail on Mum's desk. 'With a view to further investigation of a complaint against you of SEC 47 ASSAULT. TO ATTEND I/C AN APPROPRIATE ADULT.'

Rich had signed his name at the bottom, the R with a loop in it, a knot illustrated in a sailor's manual. I imagined, even in those circumstances, the pride he'd have taken in being asked to sign his name at the foot of an official form, The Principal.

Mum drove to the centre and took Richard to the local police station. A constable led them past cells to an interview room. He said the interview would be recorded. Mum said Richard was at the centre in part because of aggressive behaviour associated with brain damage. She said he'd had a bad seizure in May; his drugs had been changed; he'd hit the fellow resident while his medication was changing. The constable described the incident.

'Do you remember doing this?' he asked.

'To be quite honest,' Richard said, 'I don't remember much.'

o

In 1920, Hans Berger at the University of Jena began his attempts to record the electrical activity in the human brain. In his first report 'On the Electroencephalogram of Man', published in 1929, Berger credited Richard Caton's experiments on rabbits and monkeys, referring particularly to his success in recording 'distinct current oscillations' in the animals' brains using electrodes and a galvanometer. Berger then described his own attempts to record the electrical signals in a human brain. Using a double-coil galvanometer and subcutaneous needle electrodes, he tried to record the electrical activity in the brain of his teenage son Klaus, his hair cut as short as possible to avoid interfering with the electrodes' contact on the scalp.

Berger's equipment produced three readings, or 'curves'. At the bottom of the paper, a small, regular wave showed the time in tenths of a second. Above it, a series of spikes interspersed with almost-flat lines showed the boy's heartbeat: his electrocardiogram. The topmost curve showed the signals picked up by electrodes attached to Klaus's scalp: the record of electrical goings-on in his brain.

Berger proposed the name *electroencephalogram* for the curve he had demonstrated for the first time in human beings. 'We see in the electroencephalogram,' he wrote, 'a concomitant phenomenon of the continuous nerve processes which take place in the brain, exactly as the electrocardiogram represents a concomitant phenomenon of the contractions of the individual segments of the heart.'

As well as recording his son's and his own EEG, Berger experimented on a series of volunteers. Out of fourteen, only one was a woman: 'the dense hair,' Berger explained, 'prevents the attachment of the electrodes.' He saw that an EEG was composed of two distinct types of waves, one large, one small: he called them alpha waves and beta waves. He observed that if one of his subjects opened their eyes during the recording, there was an immediate change in the waves of the EEG. If he challenged his subject with mental arithmetic, the EEG showed the same change. Mid-way through recording the waves of his thirty-year-old assistant,

Berger touched his subject's hand with a glass rod. A fraction of a second later, the EEG curves changed dramatically: the alpha waves disappeared, replaced by a series of much smaller beta waves. With different subjects, Berger fired a cap pistol, or pricked their hand without warning, or simply asked them to open their eyes: in each case, the sensory stimuli caused changes in the EEG patterns.

Berger published fourteen reports 'On the Electroencephalogram of Man'. He recorded the brain waves of his fourteen-year-old daughter, Ilse; of volunteers to whom he'd administered chloroform, anaesthetics, caffeine or cocaine; of a boy aged thirty-five days; of schizophrenic patients and manic-depressive patients; of volunteers who'd agreed to let themselves be deprived of oxygen; and of his son Klaus both while relaxed and while challenged to multiply twenty-two by forty-three. As Klaus attempted to solve the problem, the alpha waves in his EEG curve diminished and in some places disappeared. Beta waves, Berger concluded, 'must be regarded as the material concomitant phenomena of *mental* processes.'

He had recorded the act of thinking.

'In the characteristic potential curve of the EEG of man,' Berger writes, 'which is composed of the action currents of the various nerve cell layers and is woven into a homogeneous whole, *the total physiological and psychophysiological activity* of the human brain finds its visible expression.' Berger added that the EEGs of people with epilepsy were often different from those of his other subjects, and suggested that by these pronounced, large oscillations 'the EEG expresses graphically the presence of the existing predisposition to seizures of the cerebrum.' Using Berger's techniques, researchers soon found that seizures were invariably accompanied by changes in the electrical activity of the brain.

o

I knew it was a bad period: I saw Richard's moods and seizures; I heard about trouble at the centre; I saw Mum and Dad at their desks, writing letters to doctors and health authorities. But I didn't get involved in the details of Richard's illness and care. My parents never forced them on me. I had my own life. I was busy at school, my head full of work, sport, music and plays; I had a teenager's friendships and conflicts to deal with, and exams to worry about, and anyway I was used to the wildness of my brother's attacks and the way his presence could shift like a weather from gentleness to threat, the thundercloud expression sliding into his face, and then shift again, his hand on your shoulder a benevolent singling-out, a bestowal of trust and favour.

He'd stopped having lunch on Wednesdays, because that was his day for washing up. He hadn't had lunch, he argued, so why should he wash up?

'The others washed up for you on all the other days.'

'Well, that's their fault.'

Even Mum and Dad couldn't say what provoked his mood swings. But football was often involved. The psychologist checked the football scores on Saturday so she'd have an idea what she'd be up against on Monday morning. Richard liked her.

'She's like red roses, shining, in a way,' he said.

He'd get up early on his birthday, appearing in the kitchen freshly shaved and washed, hair brushed, eyes sparkling, a celebration lustre I recognized from Easter and Christmas, when it seemed the day had found in Richard a means of announcing its distinction. This August evening he wore his suit with a waistcoat and black bow tie, his pipe cupped in his left hand; he looked on as we laid the table in the Dining Room, one of the house's formal public spaces, a medieval undercroft with a vaulted stone ceiling, oak linenfold panelling round the walls. Mum put candles in the middle of the round rosewood table; Rich extended his Zippo with a flame ready before she'd even pulled her hand away. The twins are here, our uncle and aunt too, Rich like a visiting head of state, guest of honour, proud and courteous, pulling a chair out for Mum and then pushing it beneath her with an excess of enthusiasm, the chair ramming her knees forward so she sits down before she's had a chance to think about it.

'You're such a good host, Richard,' our aunt says. 'You really are a gentleman.'

'Well,' he replies, pride and bashfulness sparring in his face, 'I don't know about that!'

Voices sound different in this old room's wood and stone acoustic. Rich lights his pipe, draws in deeply and exhales: a cloud drifts over the table, tethered by ropes of darker candle smoke.

'Do you remember the *Cautionary Tales*, Rich?' Dad asked.

'What, you mean Hilaire Belloc?'

'That's it.'

'I do, yes,' Richard said. 'I wouldn't forget them, would I, Mum?'

'I don't think you would. Do you remember Jim?'

'"There was a boy whose name was Jim,"' he began, in a low, steady voice, an actor slipping into performance register. '"His friends were very good to him . . ."'

We all stopped talking and looked at Richard.

'"They gave him tea, and cakes, and jam, and slices of delicious ham . . ."'

He recited slowly, in an even tone, the lines drawn out, their rhythm emphasized, pride shining in his face, the whole table's attention focused on him, his eyes twinkling with candlepoints. He kept reciting, looking round at each of us in turn as Jim slipped his nurse's hand at the zoo and ran away.

'"He hadn't gone a yard when – Bang!

With open jaws, a lion sprang,

And hungrily began to eat

The boy: beginning at his feet . . ."'

Now everyone round the table was smiling. Nobody

took their eyes off Richard. He kept going, without hesitation or stumble, word-perfect. How had he remembered all this? I didn't know anything as substantial by heart. The whole poem was intact in a safe corner of his brain, a nugget in a seam of ore.

'"Now just imagine how it feels
When first your toes and then your heels,
And then by gradual degrees,
Your shins and ankles, calves and knees,
Are slowly eaten, bit by bit.
No *wonder* Jim detested it!"'

I didn't remember the poem. I'd never heard Richard recite it before. I found myself held in a double suspense, both wondering how the story was going to turn out and if Richard's memory would carry him through to the end. I didn't know what was going to happen as the zookeeper ordered the lion to put Jim down. But it's too late, the lion has eaten all the way to Jim's head, and Richard's grin broadens and glows as he reaches the last line and we all break into applause. He's proud to be at the centre of such acclaim but embarrassed by the attention, and I can see the happy tension in his face again, not sure if he should suppress or unleash his smile. He looks down at his plate and laughs; when he looks up, his eyes are glittering.

o

Once a year, while I was away at school, Mum and Dad or both took Rich on holiday. Afterwards he'd glue photographs

into albums with characteristic thoroughness, tongue probing his cheek; he wrote captions in rounded capital letters,
ballpoint indentations on the next page.

Some of the photos were thumb-blurred.

Madrid in February: the Prado, the Retiro Gardens, the
Palacio Real. Mum and Richard caught a bus to the Bern-
abeu Stadium and watched from the terraces as Real Madrid
beat Almería 4-1, buying peaked paper caps to keep the sun
off.

Venice. The Doge's Palace, the Campanile, the Lido, the
Rialto, St Mark's Piazza crowded with runners in tracksuits,
waiting for the Bridges Race, Richard's face lighting up as he
describes it.

'It's a race they have every year,' he said. 'You have to
cross as many bridges as you can. And do you realize, the
winner crossed forty-two bridges? Forty-two bridges!'

When they walked across a bridge, a steward handed
them plastic cups of shandy, mistaking them for competi-
tors.

Trams in Lisbon. Sintra, Cascais, Rich swimming in the
sea at Estoril, in March.

On the deck of the Mull ferry. 'What incredible *swash*!'

Long walks through Paris in November, the boy choir
rehearsing *Ave Verum* in Notre-Dame, the lift rushing them
to the top of the Eiffel Tower, fire-eaters lying on broken
glass outside the Pompidou Centre. Near the Sacré Cœur
Rich sat to have his portrait sketched by a Croatian girl.

'She took *eighteen* minutes. *Eighteen* minutes!'

'How did you keep still?'

'Well, the thing is, you have to set a point and keep looking at it.'

'What did you look at?'

'Well, I think I was rather clever, actually. I looked at her green eyeshadow.'

Copenhagen. The long curved prows of Viking ships in the museum at Roskilde. Climbing the spire at Our Saviour's Church, the staircase winding round the outside of the spire, in open air. Rich in his blue and yellow Leeds United bomber jacket at Elsinore. The Tüborg Brewery.

'And do you realize? You'll never guess. We got free bottles of beer afterwards. Free bottles!'

Richard and my father walking the cliffs at St Justinian in west Wales, the coastal path at Solva, seals slouched over the rocks at Ramsey Island. Going down into the coal pits at a mining museum near Pontypool.

Rich counting fourteen seals at Calf Island off the Isle of Man. A golf course by the Irish Sea, gulls rowdy overhead. My mother took a swing and missed.

'Even the seagulls are laughing at you!' Rich said.

The Channel Islands. Riding a horse-drawn carriage along the lanes in Sark; watching puffins; the sequin glitter of fish-shoals in clear water round Herm. Rich in a blue, white and yellow Leeds United cap among the masts and bunting of the marina at St Peter Port, Dad's old binoculars hanging off his shoulder.

Rich trying to waterski in St Aubin's Bay. Instead of

using a rope, the instructor had beginners hold on to a long metal bar that stuck from the side of the launch like a fixed oar. Rich in a sleeveless wetsuit, a red life-jacket. He couldn't master it; he couldn't keep his arms and legs straight and lean back as the launch accelerated; he kept crumpling into his own wake. But the last morning they decided to try again, and this time Rich held on while the boat's gathering speed lifted him until he was standing on top of the water, a triumph of strength rather than technique, as if he'd actually hauled himself from one element into another.

Coffee and a cigar in the hotel that evening.

On a plane to Majorca he said the clouds looked like footprints in snow.

Outside the cathedral in Barcelona, Rich in his *Soccer is Life!* T-shirt, a Leeds baseball cap, sunglasses, pipe cupped in his right hand.

Riding a camel outside Sousse, wearing a white head-scarf.

'I'm rather touched by the Tunisian deserts,' he said.

o

I dreamed I was standing at the edge of the moat, close to the mulberry tree. For a long time I didn't move. Mum was waiting on the far bank. She raised her arms away from her sides and moved them slowly up and down, as if they were wings. I understood that I was a heron, and that she was showing me what to do with my wings. The long, feathered limbs weren't strange to me. I stretched them to their full extent and raised and lowered them just as my mother had demonstrated, feeling the lift each downstroke produced, the possibility of flight. My feet left the ground and I flew under my own power, crossing the moat on a heron's steady wingbeats towards my mother on the far side.

I made longer forays into surrounding country. It used to be enough to wander the moat looking for pike in the shallows, or comb for pottery fragments among stones and fetid weed heaps in the strand above the waterline. I'd spent hours moving between the mossy throne space in the horse chestnut, the grassed-over mound of dredge-matter, the tree-shack accessed by holly branches, the bamboo and gunnera jungle by the sluice gate, the iron gantry walkway over the waterfall, the house always in view. Now I walked out into the fields beyond the park – beyond the farm at Fulling Mill, following the Sor Brook towards Hazelford, along the valley too rumpled for planting. Frost had lifted a Roman stone coffin to the surface here, and the presence of this ancient grave conferred a kind of holiness on the place, so that just to climb the loose-jointed timber gate and take your first steps into the field was to experience a stretching of temporal and spiritual perspectives.

The brook disappeared into a cluster of oaks, limes and hawthorns. The ruined village lay beneath the trees: unnatural mounds and hollows in the grass; the corner of a cottage, covered in ivy; remnants of a mill race, a sprawl of broken-up stonework by the water. Apart from a few nettle clumps, there's no undergrowth, and it's like walking into a cathedral nave, columns of trees fanning in high vaults overhead. I scrambled over hummocks that were houses collapsed in on themselves and turfed over; I tried to imagine the village when it was still inhabited: a hamlet of less than twenty people, three generations in the same house; carts, anvils, thatch roofs and cockerels, smells of horse dung and fire smoke, the mill wheel turning in the brook. First it had been a fulling mill, for cleaning and thickening wool, then a paper mill, all the adult men in the village employed as papermakers, and finally a corn mill. But by 1901 it had fallen out of use. The village's last inhabitants left in 1914. The mill was blown up and all the metal in it used for munitions.

On warm days I sat against the house mounds or lay on the grass. The brook coursed across stones; pigeons clattered in and out of the trees. The place lent itself to dreaminess. I went back to particular memories and guided them to different outcomes. I thought about journeys and romances. I was in Hazelford, but my mind was at the house near the sea, a friend's parents renting it, another family in the next house down the dirt track, their daughter asleep in the hammock on the shaded terrace. We had to have siestas. I lay facing the tall windows, watching the sheers luff and ripple in the breeze from the fan, salt thickness in my hair, my skin sandy brown against the white sheets. I put my headphones on and listened to songs, replaying our glances and conversations, full of longing. She'd asked if I knew how to play backgammon, and I said I'd never played it before, I didn't know the rules, the board's narrow black triangles made no sense to me. She began to explain, clicking the red and black checkers into stacks, talking about bars and anchors, the home and outer board; I nodded even when I couldn't follow; I could feel sweat beading above my lip but was still surprised when I wiped the back of my hand across and found how damp it was.

They had a pool. I'd never spent so much time in a pool. I was used to the moat's brown-green murk, coots meddling in the banks, grass snakes and pike swimming alongside and beneath me. I'd keep my mouth closed against surprise flotsams of duck turds and leaf mould; I'd keep as close to the surface as I could, dreading the silt and algae bottom-substance, trying not to let my feet drop: I thought if my feet sank into it I wouldn't be able to kick them free again, the invisible ooze had quicksand suction power and fed on swimmers. I loved the pool's blue transparency and clean smooth planes, and the way, after a dive, she surfaced slowly with her head angled so the water swept her hair back from her face, her eyes closed as if she was savouring each return to the sun, or as if she knew someone was watching.

'Do you want to see round the house?' I asked when she came to visit.

'OK,' she said.

I opened the door in the music room. We walked in

silence down the Groined Passage into the Great Hall. I was nervous. I heard myself holding forth like a tour guide about the castle's history and features of interest. I talked about duels and banquets under film-set lights; Mum rubbing WD40 into suits of Spanish armour in the west wall niches; how I'd learned to ride a bike with the carpet as a safety mat beneath me.

She wore a white cotton shirt untucked over jeans, a fine silver chain round her neck.

'You see the shape of an arched window in the stone?' I asked. 'That's part of the old medieval house, before they extended it in the sixteenth century.'

I wanted to take her hand. My palms were damp.

'And these leather buckets are fire buckets. They're what they used for fire extinguishers in the eighteenth century.'

'Really?'

She pushed a wisp of hair behind her ear.

'Yes. They filled them with sand and left them around, just in case.'

'OK.'

I threw facts like sandbags into the silence between us. The Latin motto painted on the Oak Room's interior porch meant, *There is no pleasure in the memory of the past*. I'd heard my parents tell people it was a corruption of a line from Virgil's *Aeneid*, Aeneas speaking to his men on the shore of North Africa after their shipwreck: 'One day,' he consoled them, 'even to remember this will give pleasure.' I'd heard the corrupted version might have been a message to King Charles II after the English Civil War, because my ancestor had supported Parliament in the rebellion and didn't want the restored monarch to dwell on that failure of loyalty. But once I'd learned the original line from *The Aeneid* I saw its ghost in the words carved and painted on the interior porch. The statements contradicted each other. The corrupted sentence urged you to forget. The ghost original urged you to remember.

'I want to show you this,' I said.

She sat beside me on the sofa in front of the fireplace. I picked up the ledger from the low oak table, a facsimile copy of the sale catalogue from 4th July 1837, when the contents of the castle had been sold at auction. She moved closer to me, so she could see the pages. My mouth was dry. Sunlight poured through the Oak Room's west windows.

'I like the names of the auctioneers,' I said, pointing.

' "Messrs. Enoch & Redfern",' she read aloud.

We browsed the book together. Hard to believe the house had once contained such riches, or that they'd been dispersed in all directions so abruptly: embroidered Indian silk quilts; carpets from Brussels, Tournay, Kidderminster and Bengal; inlay marquetry cabinets, encoigneurs and tables; superb ormolu and other clocks; large-fold Indian screens, old Japan cabinets and Nankin china dinner sets; rare ancient bronze medallions, medals and Roman coins; heathen idols; pieces of Beauvais Tapestry; the fin of a whale; paintings and portraits attributed to Velázquez, Van Dyke and Spagnoletti, over three hundred lots in all, items and prices and buyers' names recorded in a neat forward-slanting clerk's hand.

'"Catalogue of an Important & Highly Interesting Sale of Splendid, Unique & Ancient Property",' I read, in a grand auctioneer's voice.

'"Rich & Costly Effects of Taste & Vertu",' she continued, smiling.

'"Two Milch Cows, Bay Pony, Two Chinese Sows & Pigs, Swan with Cygnets, and Peacock."'

'"A Remarkably Fine Aloe, Eighty Years Old. A Pair of Indian Chief's Moccasins."'

'"Curious African & Indian Implements of War, Including a Full-Sized Canoe, With Paddles, Etcetera, brought to this country by Captain Cook from the Sandwich Islands."'

We were laughing. We left the room through the interior porch, beneath *There is no pleasure in the memory of the past*, and as we took the stairs to the Long Gallery I was already thinking of the rooms ahead of us, how we were on our way to the roof, the Barracks, the Captain of the Guards' Room beyond the secret door.

o

The centre had a tennis court but Rich couldn't find anyone to play tennis with. I promised I'd come on the train, with my tennis racquet, but I didn't do anything about it. I kept putting it off. Then my parents said they'd pay for the train ticket, and I didn't have any excuses. I took my bike and cycled the few miles from the station, speed bumps on the drive, red-brick buildings around rough lawns planted with apple trees and birches, clumps of pampas grass in plume shapes like ideas of fountains.

I didn't need to ask for Richard. He was the first person I saw, sitting on a tractor mower, mowing the green in the middle of the red-brick residential units. I locked my bike to a railing while Rich parked the tractor and walked towards me. He was smiling, in tweed cap, T-shirt and jeans, steel watchstrap fixed too tight round his wrist, his face and forearms tanned from outdoor work.

'Hi, Rich.'

'Hi.'

We didn't know how to greet each other, away from our common ground.

The concrete tennis court by the car park was full of cracks and divots, the net ragged, the lines faded underfoot. We didn't talk while we played, the ball making high, desultory journeys between us, and I was glad when Rich said he'd had enough and asked if I'd like to see the greenhouse, the horticulture unit he went to work in every weekday, signing the register at nine each morning, brew-times at ten and three, a long lunch break at twelve.

'You'll never guess who this is!' he said. 'It's my brother!'

Now he was beaming, pipe cupped in his left hand as he gestured with his right, introducing me to Adam, the boss, and Eric, Keiran, Patrick, David, Linda, Chris and John, some of them in helmets to prevent head injuries during seizures, some of the helmets black, with hard shells, others lightweight and soft, like the helmets worn by cycle racers.

'These are the compost sacks,' Rich said, using the pipe as a pointer. 'These are what we call the seedling plugs. And these are the workbenches.'

They were filling ornamental baskets and tubs with compost and planting them with begonias, pelargoniums, petunias and busy lizzies. Rich had been levelling the ground for a second polytunnel, flattening the gravel with a yard-whacker. He was digging a trench for the water pipe.

'I'm digging your grave, I am,' he'd told Adam. 'I'm digging your grave!'

Adam took the whole team on outings in the minibus. At the Four Oaks Garden Show Rich had noticed that the orange tree by the till was plastic.

'Disgraceful,' he'd said. 'It's an absolute disgrace.' He shook his head. 'A plastic plant? It's a disgrace.'

Adam drove them to the castle, to see the garden.

'Is this your house, then, Richard?' Keiran asked him. 'Not too bad, I suppose.'

Rich smiled, pride like a light switched on inside him, a glow. The long mixed borders brimmed with life and colour. The team walked along them at their various paces, Mum and Dad pointing out plants, saying their names. Everyone stopped to admire a sunflower.

'A sunflower, yes,' Rich said. 'In the heat and the joy of the sun.'

They were just reaching the corner of the west border when Eric had a fit and crashed into a mature hebe shrub, his body rigid in the tonic phase. The whole bush shook as he convulsed, Adam kneeling beside him on the lawn. When Eric got to his feet again we all saw the canyon he'd made in the hebe: it seemed to have split into two smaller shrubs.

'That's all right, Eric,' Rich said, his hand on Eric's shoulder. 'We'll look after you.'

o

The ironstone was crumbling, mullions and battlement topstones losing definition. Deathwatch beetles infested the timbers: the roof beams were riddled with galleries. Dad kept disappearing to the draughty room off the west stairs to do sums, go over reports and apply for grants. In the autumn a local stonemason called Peter Hillman arrived with his apprentice Mark Faulkner to set up scaffolding round the Oak Room and Great Parlour. They brought ironstone from a quarry used by the house's original builders; they extracted decayed stones from the walls and cut replacements, roughening the face with a chisel before slotting each new block in. They repaired the roof parapet, the ball kneelers, the chimney capitals and coping stones, the chapel buttresses and medieval window traceries, painting the fresh stones with a mixture of soot, yoghurt and manure to be an appealing growth-medium for lichens and mosses.

I went away to boarding school; I came home to the moat, gatehouse, church and park. I chatted to Bert and Mrs Dancer, Mrs Green, Mrs Upton, Joyce, Harry Bennett and Peter Hillman. I walked further and further afield, out to Hazelford, or to Jester's Hill, Crouch Hill and Madmarston Hill, pushing out the limit of my home range, following the Sor Brook, cricket-bat willows spaced along it like streetlamps. When Rich came home we might play cricket together or practise slip catches, but more often I'd go off on my own, cross the bridge into a freedom of options, walks in all directions, the barns off the farm track towards Tadmarton, the hollow veteran ash by Fulling Mill, the hens going in and out of their sheds on gangplanks fretted like guitar necks.

The rooks were always there, in the treetops across the moat, their caws a default sound the brain learned to filter out, so that it took a sudden flurry of rooks rising from the tree-tops – or for you to be walking across the lawn in early evening when rooks returned from the fields, an armada of birds approaching from the west – for that noise to brim over into your awareness, for the rooks to make themselves heard again. I imagined the island to be watched over by rooks and herons. I'd started to define one bird against the other. It wasn't just that they were different species. They seemed ambassadors from different kingdoms: the rooks sociable, noisy, restless; the heron solitary, silent, contemplative. They suggested two entirely different modes of being, a choice of how to live in the world.

Mum passed me a letter from one of her friends. The letter was full of news of her daughter, who was spending a year teaching in Africa before she went to university, and there was a photocopy attached to it, a long report written by the girl, describing life at the school, the dust and heat, the yellow acacia trees, the characters of her pupils and colleagues. I read about her adventures with a pang of envy. I wanted to have them too. She wasn't much older than me, and I wanted to know how she'd found a job like that, so far away. Mum's friend sent details of the organization; I applied for a position; after two rounds of interviews I learned that I'd been accepted. I was going to teach for a year in the north-east of Brazil, in a region I'd never heard of. My employers were expecting me at the end of July, three weeks after I left school. I was seventeen.

o

In 1928, the neurosurgeon Wilder Penfield moved to Montreal to be Professor of Neurosurgery at McGill University and Surgeon-in-Charge of Neurosurgery at the Royal Victoria Hospital. Penfield had been a student of Charles Sherrington's in Oxford; he'd travelled to Madrid to learn the silver-staining technique directly from Santiago Ramón y Cajal and his colleague Pio del Rio-Hortega; he'd been to Breslau in Germany to watch the surgeon Otfrid Foerster operate on the brains of conscious patients with focal epilepsy, noting the way Foerster 'treated the brain with a sort of reverent gentleness.'

In Montreal, working alongside the electroencephalographer Herbert Jasper, Penfield would operate on more than seven hundred and fifty patients suffering from epilepsy. In many cases, the cause of a patient's seizures couldn't be identified. But in others, Penfield and Jasper used the EEG to locate an originating focus – a scar or tumour – from which the disorderly, paroxysmal electrical discharge emerged. Penfield found that he was often able to produce, by electrical stimulation, the same sensation experienced by the patient immediately before a seizure. Once they isolated the seizure focus, they could consider removing it surgically.

In *Epilepsy and the Functional Anatomy of the Human Brain*, published in 1954, Penfield and Jasper describe the case of a twelve-year-old boy who'd been having seizures since he was nine. The boy said his attacks were usually preceded by a hallucination of coloured triangles placed irregularly over each other, and of a robber coming after him with a gun. His EEG showed abnormality in his brain's right occipital lobe during the onset of a seizure. Under local anaesthetic, Penfield removed part of the boy's skull, exposing much of his brain's right hemisphere. Using a finely calibrated electrode, the surgeon stimulated points of the patient's cortex, and recorded his reactions. The boy couldn't see what was going on: 'He had no means of knowing when the stimulating electrode was applied to the cortex unless he was told.'

When Penfield applied small electric impulses to the

temporal lobe, the boy began to report auditory memories: 'My mother is telling my aunt over the telephone to come up and visit us tonight,' he said. 'My mother is telling my brother he has got his coat on backwards. I can just hear them.' When Penfield touched the electrode to the boy's occipital lobe, he reported a pricking sensation in the thumb of his left hand. Then, after Penfield applied a tiny electric shock to another point, the boy said: 'There it is, the same thing that I got with the spells.'

He saw red, yellow, blue and orange triangles.

'The triangles again,' he said. 'They were in front of me.'

Penfield applied another small-voltage shock.

'Oh gee!' the boy exclaimed. 'Gosh! Robbers coming at me with guns.'

Penfield touched the electrode onto the brain again.

'Oh gosh!' the boy said. 'There they are, my brother is there, he is aiming an air rifle at me.'

Penfield found a lesion in the same area of the occipital lobe, the brain 'yellow and rough'. Jasper's EEG showed maximum electrographic disturbance in the same part of the brain.

Penfield and Jasper go on to describe the case of a twenty-six-year-old woman who'd been having seizures since she was five or six. Jasper's EEG indicated that the epileptic focus was situated deep in the right temporal lobe. The woman said her seizures were preceded by an aura – a feeling in her sternum like sudden fear, or, she said, 'where you feel *happiness*'. Penfield removed part of her skull under local anaesthetic, exposing the right temporal lobe. Again, using a Rahm stimulator, he gave tiny electric shocks to a series of points on the brain. The woman reported a tingling in her left thumb, a jumping sensation on the left side of her lower lip. Then, when Penfield stimulated the undersurface of the temporal lobe, the woman reported her 'funny feeling': the sensation she always had before a seizure. Penfield touched the electrode to a nearby spot.

'I hear some music,' the woman said.

The surgeon applied the stimulator once more.

'I heard the music again,' she said. 'It's like the radio.'

'While the electrode was held in place,' Penfield and Jasper would report, 'the patient hummed the air passing from chorus to verse while all in the operating room waited in silence. Then the operating nurse, Miss Stanley, interrupted.'

'I know it,' Miss Stanley said. 'It's "Rolling Along Together".'

'Yes,' the patient said. 'Those words are in it but I don't know whether that is the name of the song.'

o

School finished. I started to count down the days to Brazil. When the house was open I sat on the bridge, selling tickets and guidebooks, or wore a GUIDE badge and stood in the Gallery, the Council Chamber or the Oak Room, answering questions, hands clasped behind my back, asking children if they wouldn't mind not clambering on the chaise-longue or plucking the loose-strung harp or tipping the blue and white china vases. I sat in the kitchen with Joyce. I walked to Fulling Mill, Hazelford and the Great Ground, to the dairy buildings, the cricket-bat willows at Miller's Osiers, the hollow ash in the Shoulder of Mutton. I walked up the hill and stood in front of Thomas's headstone. I said good-bye to my first places.

I made packing lists and laid out clothes and books in orderly piles across the bedroom floor. Things were moving so quickly: I didn't even have a guidebook to Brazil. I pictured rainforests and glittering bays, spinning out daydreams of exotic love affairs as I walked to Frederick's Wood and along the farm track towards Tadmarton, keeping close to the hedges for the shade. Yellowhammers sang in the hedges. A glider rode a thermal against the blue. The sheep grazing the park had just been sheared and their fresh-cropped fleeces looked like the pith under orange skins, the silvery grey-green cricket-bat willows along the brook shimmering when wind disturbed them. The air hummed with insects. Sometimes I stopped and turned to look back towards the house: the spire and castle chimneys bleached, bone-white, the park's trees deep green, the wheat fields beyond them ripened to sandy yellow in the mesh of hedgelines. When I started walking again all my attention swung inwards, fantasies of Brazil coursing through me. I passed the old barn with the owl's nest in it without noticing.

The sound startled me, wind screaming off hard angles and surfaces. The glider that had seemed so far away had lost height; now it was flying low, right over my head, and in an instant I saw cockpit glass, lines of rivets in white panels, the little wheel half-hidden in the fuselage. I'd never seen a glider this close. I thought it was going to crash; I was ready to run for help from Fulling Mill. But then the craft completed a final turn and came down in Quarry Ground in front of me, a long sibilance like water on shingle as thousands of barley whiskers brushed the body and wings, and then stalks bore the weight, cushioning the smooth, whale-like belly and taper. The glider came to a halt, the wingtip nearest me touching the ground like someone putting out one hand for balance. The grey Perspex hatch opened. A man eased himself out, jumped down and waded towards me through the crop. He wore sunglasses, jeans, a red polo shirt with a flying-club shield on the breast.

'Afternoon,' he said.

'Afternoon.'

'I came down a bit short, I'm afraid. Do you know where I could find a telephone?'

I pointed him towards the farm.

'Cheers,' he said, raising his right hand in acknowledgement as he turned and set off along the edge of the field, his white plane gleaming.

o

Martin and Susannah came back on my last afternoon to see me off; Richard was already home for his summer holiday. We went out in the punt, Rich in the gondolier role at the stern, watching for herons. He lit the candles on the almond-shaped table before we sat down for supper. I was too excited to be afraid. I wasn't sad: I was thinking about what I was going towards, not what I was leaving behind.

That evening, I walked in the garden. Just after nine o'clock, a half-moon lifting in the south-west. The trees were still. Rooks were flying in from the park; swifts were wheeling over the house. Mist rose off the moat, the air cooling more quickly than the water, a swan emerging like a source of light, a sea phosphorescence glowing in the dusk, staghead oaks and Dad's young trees in protective pens beyond it. I could hear rooks cawing, sheep braying in the park, wing-flurries in the rhubarb and bamboo jungle by the sluice gate, the Sor Brook plunging off the falls. Stars were coming out. I walked through the arch into the Ladies' Garden, into roses and lavender, and went down the uneven stone steps to the spring – a fairy dell of mosses, ferns, spleenwort and watercress, a shrine devoted to water, the bottom steps slippery with invisible algal coatings. The house's plumbing drew from this source, and that water tasted different – purer, closer to the origins of water – from any other I ever drank. I dipped my hand into it. I walked back through the arch and stood on the lawn, looking up at the French windows behind the iron balcony. The lamps were on and I could see Rich standing in the windows. We waved at each other. I walked to the edge of the moat. The park's trees were silhouettes, like cut-outs. A contrail hung in a long diagonal over the Great Ground. The swifts had gone. The sky was empty for a few minutes before the first bats appeared. The house was bathed in silver light. I stood on the grass near the water. I tried to take it all in. I wanted to make it part of me. I wanted to carry it with me when I went away.

FOUR

'ARE WE GOING TO say a prayer in the Chapel?' Richard asked one evening.

He was sitting in the green chair, pipe cupped in his left hand.

'Yes, if you'd like to, Rich,' Dad said. 'Let's do that.'

Rich opened the door and stepped into the cold stone room. He took the Zippo from his trouser pocket as he approached the altar; he lit the two cream-white candles like a monk carrying out an ancient duty.

The leather-bound covers of the Chapel's hymnals and prayer books were coming loose. Mum had ripped an old blue pillowcase into thin strips and tied one round each book's midriff to hold the sections together. These venerable books stood in a row beneath the stained-glass window in the north wall, and in their cotton belts with the ends tied in bows the books looked as if they were wearing dressing gowns. The Chapel's silence had always made me nervous. That silence had particular density, as if the Chapel had gathered surplus quiet and stillness from every other room in the house and stored them up against shortage. But it never seemed to bother Mrs Green. She polished the plain brass cross and candlesticks on the stone altar; she dusted the wooden pews and the rudimentary font where I'd been christened; she used a brush attached to several lengths of garden cane to bring down cobwebs from the vaulted ceiling, manoeuvring the rod with her head tilted back, gazing up as if she were brushing webs from the lunar craters.

On New Year's Day just before eleven o'clock the vicar arrived with a small black suitcase full of communion gear: a silver chalice, a silver box for wafers, two stoppered glass jugs for wine and water. Men and women came down the hill from the village, enlarged and softened in wool coats, jumpers, scarves and hats, the Chapel transformed by voices and body temperatures. Richard was in his element, welcoming each new arrival, ushering them into pews, passing out prayer books, his voice ringing above the low congregation hubbub, his amens and other responses lagging one syllable behind, an echo drawing strength from its circuit of the walls.

Afterwards, he led the way downstairs and showed the visitors into the kitchen. Mum made mugs of coffee. Rich offered round a plate of biscuits. He set his right hand on Mrs Field's shoulder and raised the biscuits into full view.

'Are you sure you don't want another?' he said. 'Just one more. Go on. Please. I think you can manage another!'

'Aren't you going to have some coffee, Richard? There's one left there, look.'

'I am, yes. But I think I'm going to have one in my Leeds mug.'

They were playing that afternoon; the mug's appearance was auspicious.

'That's right, we're playing Liverpool. At home. And do

you realize, it's Alan Clarke's four-hundredth game for Leeds! *Four-hundredth!*'

o

Richard's days found a more even keel. Drugs reduced the frequency and severity of his seizures. Members of staff at the centre understood and valued him. The fights and violent outbursts seemed things of the past. He loved his job in the horticultural unit, his music and singing, his pipe, his holidays with Mum and Dad, his visits home. Leeds were winning again, his bedroom decked in blue and gold.

He was forty-one when a night seizure stopped him breathing.

I was abroad, and didn't get Martin's message until after dark.

'Rich died this morning,' he said simply. 'Come and join us.'

The bishop who'd confirmed Richard gave the address at his service. The bishop had been born in Leeds, within a mile of Elland Road. He remembered the roar that came up over the hill whenever the home side scored a goal. He said that life was given us for brightness. Richard, he said, 'reached out for the bright thing.'

Richard was buried beside Thomas. 'We are rich in what we have lost,' my mother said, in the kitchen. She wasn't sure where the words had come from, but she kept repeating them, hearing his name in them: 'We are *rich* in what we have lost. We are *rich*.'

It was just after Easter. For days we heard a bird cannon booming from the Great Ground. Trees were coming into leaf. Fields of oil-seed rape were starting to yellow. Each spring, when the daffodils were over, Dad would go round the moat with a spade to split clumps of the bulbs. He'd take one half of a clump and dig it in further along the bank, spreading the show of flowers year by year. Now I took a spade from Bert's shed too and walked round past the sluice gate to join him. Dad was past eighty, but he seemed to have more energy than I did, the two of us standing on our spades' shoulders, forcing the blades through the crust of turf, splitting the bulbs, planting the half-clumps, tamping the earth down over them, using divots to fill the holes we left behind. We didn't say anything while we dug and moved the daffodils, the rooks working on their nests above us, flying in from the park carrying long sticks like pole-vaulters, a heron stationed beneath the oak where Harry Bennett's tree house was a few rotten planks overgrown with ivy.

The moat froze almost every year when I was younger. Each morning I'd go down the stone steps to the water by the front door and test the ice, tapping and then stamping my foot on it, until one day I left the steps altogether and trusted my whole weight to the freeze. But my father still wouldn't give the go-ahead: when he trod on the ice I heard groans and other sounds like sonar plinks on submarines moving away from us – hairline fissures, air bubbles shifting beneath the layer. I understood that the ice was still fallible and I'd have to wait. Then one morning Rich and Dad would stand on the steps by the moat together. Because Rich was the heaviest, and because he'd savour the responsibility of testing the ice officially, of being trusted with the final say, Dad gave him the task of jumping up and down, as hard as he could. The ice must have been inches thick by now and Richard's weight didn't trouble it.

Already he'd gone up to the Barracks and found the cardboard box of brown and black leather skates, steel runners clanking as he carried the box downstairs, the runners toothed on their curved tips for purchase on the ice when you went up on your toes, a ladder and life-ring on the grass in case of emergency. I was impatient to pull on old socks and lace the boots up, double bows pulled tight: I wanted to be first on the ice, especially if snow had fallen, the moat flawless white, the sound of the runners muffled when you skated out, muscles waking up in the calves, rooks and jackdaws carousing overhead. I turned and watched my mother and the twins step out onto the moat, and then Richard too, his face set in stern concentration, his mouth open, a bulge in his cheek where his tongue probed unconsciously. He pushed off with his right foot, moving awkwardly, arms held out like a scarecrow's, relying on strength rather than technique to keep him upright, as if skating was a contest in which you fought with ice and gravity. He wore his thin leather jacket with his Leeds United scarf tucked in, and his Leeds United bobble hat, dots of gold and blue moving on the snow. Suddenly his skates got away from under him and his upper body thudded shoulder-first into the ice. He lay spreadeagled and for a moment he didn't move, but then he raised his head and saw that we'd all stopped to look at him.

'I'm all right!' he said. 'Don't worry! I'm all right!'

He got to his feet and brushed the snow off his jacket and trousers.

On summer afternoons I'd wait for Dad to finish work and walk back in under the gatehouse from the office by the kitchen gardens, folders under his arm. I'd sit in front of the house with my cricket bat and ball, watching the gatehouse arch, and as soon as he came back we'd go onto the west lawn and Dad would take his jumper off and drop it on the grass to mark the bowler's wicket. I'd tap the toe of the bat on the ground as I'd seen batsmen do on television, waiting for my father to take his short run-up and bowl, the park sloping up behind him toward Stafford Wood, each ball emerging from the green of old oaks and chestnuts. The lawn was bounded on three sides by areas of rough ground where Bert let the grass grow, and it was a thrill to hit the ball cleanly and see it disappear across that boundary. Sometimes Dad came closer and threw the ball again and again at the same spot of ground so I could rehearse particular strokes, trying to keep my feet, shoulders and hands in correct relation to one another, trying to bring out into the day shapes and gestures that already existed in my mind's eye, trying to close the gap between the perfect movement I could see clearly in my imagination and the actual figure my body made in the world. Sometimes Richard played with us too. I got nervous if he took the ball to bowl at me. He didn't mean to send the ball down too fast for me to deal with or hurl it back too hard for Dad to catch when he retrieved it from the longer grass, but he didn't know his own strength, and he couldn't always portion it appropriately to particular actions.

For a while Rich learned the double bass, bowing at the cables like a sawyer. But the challenge of converting printed marks into precise physical configurations proved too complicated, and he soon lost patience. A local church organist agreed to give him singing lessons at the centre. Once a week they met in a room next to the laundry, an upright piano against one wall, slatted shelves and airing frames against the other. Rich arrived in his Leeds bobble hat and scarf, his leather music case bulging with Gilbert and Sullivan scores; he carried his pipe in his free hand and set it down carefully on top of the piano before removing his jacket and Leeds trimmings.

I'd hear him singing in church on Sunday mornings. He had a clear, soft baritone voice but he sang with a slight lag, as if he were hearing the music on a long-distance line across time zones: at intervals he'd recognize the lag's existence and rush to make good the discrepancy.

His teacher suggested they try some scales, arpeggios and other exercises.

'I don't really want to do that,' Rich said.

He wanted to sing Gilbert and Sullivan, his vocal scores for *Iolanthe*, *HMS Pinafore* and *The Gondoliers* marked with

breathing prompts and other reminders. He wanted to sing
Welsh hymns like 'Guide Me, O Thou Great Redeemer' and
'Love Divine, All Loves Excelling', and other Welsh songs
like 'The Land of My Fathers', 'All Through the Night'
and 'God Bless the Prince of Wales'. He sang a carol called
'Joy to the World'. He sang 'Sweet Little Buttercup' as a duet
with his teacher, Rich teasing her when she couldn't reach
the high notes.

'It might be good if you could expand your repertoire a
little bit,' she suggested.

'What should I want to do that for?' he said.

He told Mum that whenever he sang Handel's 'Silent
Worship' he thought about her:

> Did you not hear my lady
> Go down the garden singing?

He sang in the music room. Often he started too low
or too high, and when the melody got away from his range
he'd change key like someone shifting gear in a car so he
could keep a grip on the tune. Sometimes, in the evening,
inspired, he'd dress up in suit, waistcoat and bow tie, and
stand in the music room with the score held out in front of
his chest just as a professional would, the Anglepoise at full
extension over his shoulder. He has an actor's feel for stage-
craft, and even after we've fallen silent he leaves a pause,
waiting for our concentration to settle and focus, our uncle
glancing up from the piano, waiting for Richard's signal.
It's Christmas; he's going to sing an anthem called 'Lead Me,
Lord'; his expression is solemn, as if a great responsibility has

been entrusted to him. He looks out over his audience. Nobody moves. The piano begins, and as the moment approaches for Rich to start singing he's like a diver gathering himself on the high board, chest expanded, on the brink of open air. We all hold our breath as he breathes in.

THANK YOU

My mother and father. Martin and Susannah.

The staff, residents and friends of the
David Lewis Centre for Epilepsy, especially
Dr Loukie Beech, Adam Cowell, Dr Geoffrey Hammond,
Pat Kelly, Helen Beck and Vivian East.

Deborah Rogers, Peter Straus, Camilla Elworthy,
Andrew Kidd and Kate Harvey.

Dr Judy Bogdanor, Dr Richard Boyd, Dr Yvonne Hart,
Mr Richard Stacey and Professor Alwyn Lishman.

Ben and Emily Faccini, Dominic Oliver, Mark Haddon,
Clare de Vries, Jon and Elaine Ronson, Nat and Niki Segnit,
Sonali Wijeyaratne, Wendy Tiffin, Lydia Rainford,
Hannah Westland, Mohsen Shah, Beatrice Monti,
Amy Gadney, Clare Reihill, Nayla Elamin, Elisa Sesti,
Dione Gibson, Kate Mayhew, Sarah Blagden,
John and Susanna White, Judy Daish and Richard Reed.

The staff and benefactors of the
British Library, the Wellcome Institute, and the
Rockefeller Medical Library, Queen Square.

Cara Denman quoted Jung to me:
'The beloved dead are our task.'

Acknowledgements

The Music Room draws on the following books and papers:

Brazier, Mary A. B., 1961, *A History of the Electrical Activity of the Brain: The First Half-Century*, London: Pitman.

Brazier, Mary A. B., 1984, *A History of Neurophysiology in the Seventeenth and Eighteenth Centuries*, New York: Raven Press.

Brazier, Mary A. B., 1988, *A History of Neurophysiology in the Nineteenth Century*, New York: Raven Press.

Cannon, Dorothy F., 1949, *Explorer of the Human Brain: The Life of Santiago Ramón y Cajal*, New York: Henry Schuman.

Caton, Richard, 1875, 'The electric currents of the brain', *British Medical Journal*, 2, p. 278.

Critchley, Macdonald, and Critchley, Eileen A., 1998, *John Hughlings Jackson: Father of English Neurology*, Oxford: OUP.

Eadie, Mervyn J., and Bladin, Peter F., 2001, *A Disease Once Sacred: A History of the Medical Understanding of Epilepsy*, Eastleigh: John Libby & Co.

Engel, Jr, Jerome, 1989, *Seizures and Epilepsy*, Philadelphia: F. A. Davis.

Engel, Jr, Jerome, and Pedley, Timothy A. (eds.), 1998, *Epilepsy: A Comprehensive Textbook*, Philadelphia: Lippincott-Raven.

Ferrier, David, 1876, *The Functions of the Brain*, London: Smith, Elder & Co.

Finger, Stanley, 2000, *Minds Behind the Brain*, Oxford: OUP.

Fuster, Joaquín M., 1997, *The Prefrontal Cortex: Anatomy, Physiology, and Neuropsychology of the Frontal Lobe*, Philadelphia: Lippincott-Raven (3rd Edition).

Gloor, Pierre, 1969, *Hans Berger on the Electroencephalogram of Man*, Amsterdam: Elsevier.

Goldberg, Elkhonon, 2001, *The Executive Brain: Frontal Lobes and the Civilized Mind*, Oxford: OUP.

Harlow, J. M., 1848, 'Passage of an iron rod through the head', *Boston Medical and Surgical Journal*, 39, pp. 383–393.

Harlow, J. M., 1868, 'Recovery from the passage of an iron bar through the head', *Publications of the Massachusetts Medical Society*, 2, pp. 327–346.

Hoft, Hebbel E., 1936, 'Galvani and the pre-Galvanian electrophysiologists', *Annals of Science*, Vol. 1, No. 2, pp. 157–172.

Hopkins, Antony, 1985, *Epilepsy: The Facts*, Oxford: OUP.

Jones, E. G., 1994, 'The Neuron Doctrine 1891', *Journal of the History of Neuroscience*, 3, pp. 3–20.

Kellaway, Peter, 1946, 'The part played by electric fish in the early history of bioelectricity and electrotherapy', *Bulletin of the History of Medicine*, 20, pp. 112–137.

Lewis, Jefferson, 1981, *Something Hidden: A Biography of Wilder Penfield*, Toronto: Doubleday.

Lishman, W. Alwyn, 1998, *Organic Psychiatry: The Psychological Consequences of Cerebral Disorder*, Oxford: Blackwell Science (3rd Edition).

Moller, Peter, 1995, *Electric Fishes: History and Behaviour*, London: Chapman & Hall.

Morgan, James P., 1982, 'The first reported case of electrical stimulation of the human brain', *Journal of the History of Medicine*, 37, pp. 51–65.

Nicholls, John G., Martin, A. Robert, Wallace, Bruce G., Fuchs, Paulo A., 2001, *From Neuron to Brain*, Sunderland, MA: Sinaver (4th Edition).

Acknowledgements

O'Leary, James L., and Goldring, Sidney, 1976, *Science and Epilepsy: Neuroscience Gains in Epilepsy Research*, New York: Raven Press.

Penfield, Wilder, and Jasper, Herbert, 1954, *Epilepsy and the Functional Anatomy of the Human Brain*, London: J. & H. Churchill Ltd.

Pera, Marcello, 1997, *The Ambiguous Frog: The Galvani–Volta Controversy on Animal Electricity*, Princeton: Princeton University Press.

Piccolino, Marco, and Bresadola, Marco, 2002, 'Drawing a spark from darkness: John Walsh and electric fish', *TRENDS in Neurosciences*, Vol. 25 No. 1, pp. 51–57.

Piccolino, Marco, 2003, *The Taming of the Ray: Electric Fish Research in the Enlightenment from John Walsh to Alessandro Volta*, Florence: Leo S. Olschki.

Schiller, Francis, 1979, *Paul Broca: Founder of French Anthropology, Explorer of the Brain*, Berkeley: University of California Press.

Stuss, D. T., and Benson, D. F., 1986, *The Frontal Lobes*, New York: Raven Press.

Temkin, Owsei, 1971, *The Falling Sickness: A History of Epilepsy from the Greeks to the Beginnings of Modern Neurology*, Baltimore: Johns Hopkins University Press (2nd edition, revised).

Walker, W. Cameron, 1937, 'Animal electricity before Galvani', *Annals of Science*, Vol. 2, No. 1, pp. 84–113.

Young, Robert M., 1970, *Mind, Brain and Adaptation in the Nineteenth Century*, Oxford: Clarendon Press.